AN ADIRONDACK SAMPLER

Day Hikes for All Seasons

by Bruce Wadsworth

ADIRONDACK MOUNTAIN CLUB
Glens Falls, New York

Second Edition

Published by The Adirondack Mountain Club, Inc.
174 Glen Street, Glens Falls, New York 12801

Library of Congress Cataloging-in-Publication Data

Wadsworth, Bruce.
  An Adirondack Sampler.

  Includes index.
  1. Hiking--New York (State)--Adirondack Mountains--
Guide-books. 2. Adirondack Mountains (N.Y.)--
Description and travel--Guide-books. I. Title.
GV199.42.N652A348   1988   917.47'53   88-16796
ISBN 0-935272-44-5

Second edition, 1988
Printed and Bound in the United States of America

Cover design: The Design Function

Photo acknowledgements: Page 33, Lawrence King; p. 74, Robin Brown; p. 83,
Ralph Geiser; pp. 61 and 68 courtesy of the Adirondack Museum. All other
photographs, sketches and maps contributed by the author.

Contents

Rondaxe (Bald) Mountain Fire Tower, 1930

Dedication

This guidebook is dedicated to the fire tower observers of the Adirondack Park. Many trails used by the hiker exist only because they lead, or once led, to a tower manned by these memorable men and women. The strong positive feelings of many New Yorkers for their Adirondacks must, like mine, be partly due to happy memories of times spent with fire observers on mountain tops.

Since 1912, when the first fire towers were authorized, fire observers have guarded our forests. Today, air surveillance and other means of fire detection have reduced, and are continuing to reduce, their numbers. One of the saddest parts about writing this book was finding so many closed towers and foundations of removed towers on mountain peaks.

Time stands still for no one, but let us not forget the dedication and lonely service of the fire observers. These philosphers and raconteurs of the peaks did much to add color and character to the mountain experiences of those of us who were privileged to share their towers.

Acknowledgments

There are a number of changes in this new edition. In the years 1977–79, when this book was first written, it was felt that due to the nature of the trails covered exact mileages were not terribly important. DEC posted mileages were generally used. As the ADK Forest Preserve Series of trail guides evolved, however, more accurate measurements became available as various authors pushed the measuring wheel over myriad Adirondack trails. Where available, these new measurements have been used.

Initial recommendations for the outings described in this book came from the Adirondack Mountain Club's Maps and Guidebooks Committee, which had considered writing this book as a committee activity. Especially helpful was the chairman, Rev. Lawrence Cotter.

Henry Young and Peggy O'Brien made many useful suggestions for the Keene-Keene Valley section. Louis Curth offered ideas for the southern Adirondacks. The trail work of Rev. Phillip Allen on Azure Mountain was much appreciated. William Tierson of the Newcomb Campus, SUNY College of Environmental Science and Forestry, greatly facilitated matters concerning trails on that campus.

Clint Miller, Grant Cole, and Tom Lee offered technical advice on photography. Thomas Shearer (Region 5) and Charles Nevin (Region 6) of the New York State Department of Environmental Conservation went to great extremes to provide needed information concerning state lands. Doris Herwig showed endless patience in guiding a neophyte author through the intricacies of publication.

Manuscript reviewers made many valuable suggestions. The detailed recommendations of Henry Germond as editor infinitely improved the final quality of the original text.

My wife, Betty, and two children, Barbara and Peter, helped with field work and suffered through writing sessions at home. Their encouragement was a great incentive to continue a difficult task.

Finally, significant thanks must be given to the many individuals I met in the field who offered helpful comments. Members of the Schenectady Chapter of ADK were particularly willing to be of service. Fire observers, forest rangers, and park rangers all went to great lengths to be as informative as possible.

To all I extend my gratitude and thanks.

It's a great thing these days to leave civilization for awhile.''

Robert Marshall, 1937

Introduction

An Adirondack Sampler was written for many reasons. It is an introduction to that vast and marvelous region called the Adirondacks. It extends an invitation to the trails, streams, and mountains that exist within the boundaries of the largest park in the United States. For those who have little knowledge of this area, it will serve as a guide into some of the nicest places in the Adirondacks that can be reached easily on foot.

This guidebook is planned for the single-day forest traveler. Hikes found here generally can be completed in six hours or less. It is for those who are just beginning the adventure of hiking. It is ideal for family outings. Just as well, it can be used by those who have traveled the more rugged high peaks and are now seeking less challenging, but just as meaningful, journeys. The winter hiker, especially the snowshoer, will find this book useful.

The Sampler contains hikes to be found in all regions of the Adirondacks. Thus, most hikers will find that interesting trips are possible without having to drive long distances. It is not necessary, nor even often desirable, for the novice to begin his climbing experience in the high peaks around Mt. Marcy. Too often the neophyte in the high peaks finds he hasn't the stamina or the skills needed to enjoy such trips. The hikes described here will enable the beginner to gain the know-how needed in the forest. Later, when he tries those high peaks, he will be able to enjoy those trips to the fullest.

This book is for the many who simply want to enjoy the out-of-doors on a weekend. For this type of hiker, the Adirondacks are epitomized by the deer that magically appears at lakeside in the shadows of the day's end. For them the cascading brook in the springtime and the falling leaves of autumn hardwoods have more significance than a crowded trail to Mt. Marcy. A quiet place with a beautiful view encourages contemplation; a rippling stream stimulates the mind's imagination to ponder pleasurable thoughts.

Across the Adirondacks are many rippling streams merrily dancing along and hundreds of quiet trails where autumn leaves may be admired. Dozens of mountains await the occasional visitor. Thousands of ponds wait to quietly tell their stories to a listening ear. *An Adirondack Sampler* describes several such places. Go and visit them. Then, seek out your own special trails and treasure them.

7

What Do You Need?

The otherwise interested hiker is often reluctant to get out on the trail because he thinks a bewildering assortment of equipment must be obtained. Not being familiar with hiking gear, he finds the whole matter confusing. Sometimes it is not considered worth making this initial hurdle, but to be discouraged for this reason would be a great mistake. First, day hikes are not lengthy expeditions. Second, while equipment should be sturdy and dependable, it need not be expensive. Purchase equipment that will satisfy *your* needs. Third, though there are some factors that must be addressed before plunging into the forest, they are relatively few in number. They include comfort, adaptability to changing conditions, health, safety, and personal interests. Most people will find they already have several of the needed items for hiking.

Comfort. Since your feet are going to get you there, treat them kindly. Generally, the steeper the trail or the heavier the climber, the more rugged should be the footwear. Acceptable footwear should fit well, be sturdy, provide ankle support, and have good traction. Shoes or boots should be well broken in. For most of the hikes in this book, sneakers or work shoes will be quite adequate. Light or medium-weight hiking boots would be nicer to have, though. *The footwear must be commensurate with their intended use.* Sneakers may be fine on a flat dry trail of short distance, but they can become mighty uncomfortable on a muddy mountain trail that suddenly fills up with water during an unexpected deluge of rain. Many hikers wear both heavy woolen socks and a lighter pair of socks under them to reduce friction. Rest occasionally so your feet can cool off. Otherwise, they may present you with a blister to remind you to be more concerned with their welfare.

In everyday life most people don't think much about walking. They get up from the table and walk to the living room, car, or kitchen. The act is over after a dozen or so steps. Hiking is considerably different. Besides having proper footwear, it helps a great deal to have your hands free. You don't mind carrying the picnic basket from the car to the table, but don't try to carry one five miles up a mountain. Put your food, sweater, and other gear in a pack of some sort. For a short trip this may be a travel bag over the shoulder. Eventually, however, you'll want a day pack. The cost, quality, and type depends upon your needs and your body build. Size can only be determined after you know what must be carried. Late fall and winter hiking requires extra space for supplemental clothing. Many packs are compressable so that size can be altered. Generally, soft packs, rather than external frame packs, are more comfortable for day hikes. There are some light internal frame packs which are also excellent. Fifteen or twenty pounds are as much as a person can easily tote all day. Carry less if possible. Make sure the pack stitching is good and that stress points are double stitched. Try on several styles to find which type feels comfortable on *your* back. An "occasional" hiker doesn't need the same quality gear as the "every weekend" hiker whose gear will get more wear and tear. Remember, cost generally varies with quality.

Adaptability to Changing Conditions. Anyone who has spent much time in the Adirondacks has heard the old adage, "If you don't like the present weather, wait around another ten minutes and it'll change." Even when the weather doesn't change, the hiker will find it cooler in the forest than out in the meadow sun. The temperature drops and winds increase as elevation is gained. On the driest of days, you'll still get soaked if you slip while crossing a stream. It is only good sense to prepare for the likely, but it is prudent to prepare for the unlikely as well.

One of the most simple, yet practical, items for adaptability is the hat. It protects you from the sun, rain, and insects. If wet, it will help cool you on a hot day. In the rain, its brim is a blessing. Put some insect repellent around the brim and watch those pesky flies disappear. In cooler weather, wool caps are best because they'll keep you warm even when wet. Upwards to a third of your body heat can be controlled through your head. Getting warm after climbing awhile? Take your hat off. Getting cold, put one on.

Make your equipment serve many functions. You may use a poncho to help keep you warm or protect you from the wind as well as to stay dry in the rain. Those extra socks you were wise enough to carry make pretty good mittens on a chilly day. A hood is desirable on that poncho or jacket. **The key to heat control is layering. Avoid perspiration.** Start with that golf jacket or light wool shirt you have in the closet. Consider the number of combinations a vest and rain jacket can offer. Carry items that can be easily taken off or added. Make the changes as soon as your body indicates a change is needed. That heavy parka may be great for sitting in a cold stadium, but don't try to climb a mountain in one.

One more word is needed. The word is *hypothermia.* Briefly, hypothermia is a condition where heat loss exceeds the capability of the body to replace it. Body temperature decreases and death can result.

For this to happen, the air temperature need not be frigid. A high wind can quickly strip body heat away. Avoid cottons, which wick water and cause body heat loss. Use synthetics in the summer and wool in the winter. Avoid soaking your clothing with body perspiration. Remember the concept of clothing layering.

Should you or a companion find that gloves or other clothing items are being lost on the trail, stumbling is occuring while walking, shivering can't be controlled, thinking is difficult, or unusual responses occur when speaking, act without delay. Get hot food and drink into the person. High-energy, quickly digested food should be used. Get the person warmed in any manner possible.

Every hiker should be familiar with the symptoms of hypothermia and remedial action for preventing it. A good brochure on this topic is available from the Adirondack Mountain Club.

Health. The forest is not the same as home. Whenever a person's environment is changed, health considerations should be examined. Get a good night's rest before setting out on your trip. Follow that up with a good, high-energy breakfast so you'll maintain your stamina after a few hours of walking. Many hikers find it better to nibble food all through the day rather than have a single large midday meal. Hard candies, nuts, raisins and other dried fruits, sunflower seeds, granola, coconut, dried cereal, chocolate, and other readily available supermarket items make good trail food (gorp). Semi-sweet chocolate won't melt in hot weather. A fresh orange is great to have along. Avoid things that require cooking or you'll be bogged down with pots, pans, and a sore back.

You'll drink more water than normal when you hike. Don't count on finding it where you need it. Take a filled canteen or plastic jug with you. Make water refills upstream from camping sites. Select places where the water is fast flowing rather than stagnant. Use water purification procedures for Giardiasis prevention. Carry extra food. And carry those wrappers and containers out with you.

It's often said that God's only mistake was the creation of the black fly. Spring hiking necessitates use of a suitable insect repellent. The best ones all have the active ingredient N, N-diethyl-meta-toluamide. By mid-July you may be tempted to leave repellents at home, but don't do it. It's a very small item to carry for the relief provided when needed.

Carry a first aid kit. It should contain an assortment of band aids, salves, small bandages, and a small pair of scissors. An Ace bandage is nice to have if an ankle is turned. In extremely warm weather salt tablets may be needed. With heavy exertion, the body can lose essential salts and, while your food normally will replace them, it's a good idea to have the tablets available.

Should you feel a tender spot developing on your foot, care for it immediately before it becomes a blister. Moleskin patches are handy for this. Cut a small hole in the center of the patch a little larger than the sore spot. Place the patch on the skin with the hole over the tender spot. The raised patch then keeps the boot from irritating it more.

Don't forget toilet tissue. While many hiking areas have privies at campsites along the trails, don't count on one being present when you need one. Leave the trail, select an area having soft earth, and make a small hole 6-8 inches deep. Cover it with leaf litter before leaving it. Nature will take care of the rest. Be sure to avoid areas which are near waterways.

Safety. Emergencies do occur. They come unannounced. Their intensity may be greatly minimized if you are prepared for them. A few basic items can make the difference between inconvenience and disaster. Do not expect someone to appear simply because help is needed. Even if you were sensible enough to tell a neighbor or friend of your intended route of travel and your expected return time, help should not be expected for several hours.

Although it may appear difficult to become lost on the trails found in this guidebook, carry it with you anyway. It has information that will help you gain insight about your trip. In some cases maps have been included with the trail descriptions. As you take those rest breaks, open your guidebook and read from it. If you have a topographical map, orient yourself and identify points of interest that are in view. Hiking is much more than simply getting from here to there. Awaken your senses to your environment. Learn more of your heritage. Become an integral part of your surroundings.

The trails in this guide are, for the most part, well marked. It is still a good idea to take a compass along. Always check your compass direction before you begin your trip, so you'll know which way to head should you become temporarily "misplaced." Take the time to become familiar with your compass *before* you need it.

Typical Trail Marker

11

Be sure to take plenty of dry matches. A candle greatly facilitates starting a fire in wet weather. If a fire is needed, build it on a rock base to prevent starting a ground fire in organic duff.

A whistle can be very useful. Every person should have one. A lost child can panic. Teach him or her to sit down and use that whistle if separated from the party. The whistle can also be used to scare away a menacing animal. It's much safer than throwing things at it, which might cause it to attack you.

Time passes quickly when you're enjoying yourself. To avoid a return trip in the dark, do two things. Carry a watch, and carry a flashlight. Keep track of the time it takes you to cover different sections of your route and allow ample time to be off the trail before dark. Rely on the flashlight only for emergency use.

A small jackknife will have a multitude of uses. Don't wear one of those huge belt knives unless you're planning to skin a buffalo. A small jackknife with a couple different-sized blades will fill the bill.

Many hikers carry a space blanket. They are light, small, and can be very useful if you get caught out overnight. They can be extremely important if a person is seriously injured and must be kept warm.

Don't start filling your pockets with all these little items. Walking will be most unpleasant. Instead, make a ditty bag out of some scrap material and attach a drawstring to close it. Throw all the little items into the little sack and dump it into the bottom of your pack. You'll know where everything is and packing becomes a cinch.

Personal Interests. Plan to enjoy yourself. What do you like to do? Take a camera if you like photography. Perhaps a field identification guide of flowers, birds, or animal tracks will make your trip more fun. A small pair of binoculars could really make the view outstanding. Maybe you would just like to read a novel and while away the time. Whatever it is that suits your interests, tuck it away in your pack and have a good time.

Composite Listing Of Hiking Equipment

Day Pack
Compass
Food
Jackknife
Candle
Insect Repellent
Salt Tablets
Wool Sweater/Shirt
Hat
Watch
Toilet Tissue
Ditty Bag

Map (Guidebook)
Canteen
Flashlight
Matches
First Aid Kit
Water Purification Tablets
Jacket with Hood
Poncho or Other Rain Gear
Extra Socks
Whistle
Space Blanket
Personal Interest Items

Trip Difficulty

Each hike description in this guide book begins with a basic listing of information that will enable you to approximate the hike's difficulty. Distances and elevations do not require evaluation except to determine if the trips are within your capability. The data are quite accurate. Your judgment must be used to make best use of some of the other information.

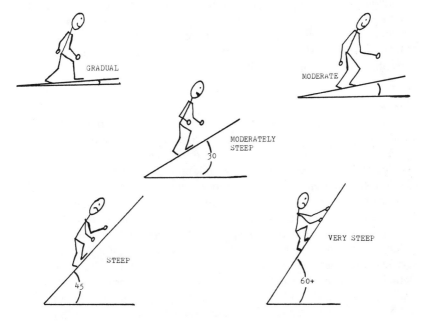

STEEPNESS   STANDARDS

Times for round trips are generally conservative. Some people walk faster than others, and even the same person may push on rapidly when a storm beckons overhead but will tarry while looking at wild flowers on a warm spring day. Are you in good physical condition? Do you have a small child along with you who may have to be carried from time to time? These are variables that must be considered. After a trip or two you should be able to compare travel times on past outings and make adjustments from the given travel times to determine the travel times that best fit your style of hiking.

What is "steep" to one person is "easy" to another. No two people seem to evaluate trail difficulty in the same manner. In the trail descriptions an attempt has been made to standardize the use of terms relating to steepness. Five terms are used. They are: gradual, moderate, moderately steep, steep, and very steep. The terms are based upon relative grade, not on ease of travel. How "easy" the grades will seem to you depends upon your physical condition, experience, and mental outlook.

Distance and Elevation

New topographic maps will be printed in metric units, while most of the maps currently in use have the English units. Therefore, distances and elevations have been expressed both in English and metric units. Metric units are placed in parentheses following the English units. The abbreviation *m* means miles in the English system and means meters in the metric system. *Km* means kilometers. One kilometer equals one thousand meters. Indicated distances have been kept to a minimum in this book. Most trips are fairly short and the intermediate distances are not really essential for following the route.

Maps

Maps are used to help you locate and follow several of the trails described in this book. These maps often include other trails not described in this book; this will permit you to gain knowledge of other places in the immediate area of the region you are hiking that may be of interest to you. Each described trail includes the topographical map quadrangles on which the trail is located. These quadrangles are 15-minute maps unless otherwise indicated. (See additional map information on page 17.)

In mapping, the term *minute* is used to represent an angle measurement. There are 60 minutes in 1 degree. There are 360 degrees in the circle encompassing the earth. A 15-minute map shows the ground area which represents 15 minutes of longitude x 15 minutes of latitude. In the Adirondacks, a 15-minute map represents a ground distance of about 12.5 m. (20 km.) in an east-west direction and about 17.5 m. (28 km.) in a north-south direction. In some cases, 7.5-minutes maps are available.

Such maps represent one fourth the ground area and one half the distances of the 15-minute map in each direction. They permit greater detail since less ground area is represented on the same size paper used for the 15-minute map.

Trail Manners

Remember that you are a visitor in a place of natural beauty. What you have come to see, others will come after you to see. The saying, "Take only pictures, leave only footprints," is an excellent motto to follow. Many hikers habitually carry litter bags and clear trails as they return after a trip. There are signs that the modern hiker is becoming more conscious of his personal obligation to maintain his natural surroundings. Set a good example.

Many trails are partially or totally on private lands. The continued use of these lands by the hiking public is often directly related to how the public uses that land. The trails and places of beauty must be kept litter free and in good condition. Do your part. If you carry it in, carry it out. When possible, also be willing to carry out litter left by others.

Campfires

There is a growing ethic that open fires should not be built in the wild except in those areas specifically established for that purpose. Lean-tos normally have fireplaces, as do certain camping areas. Remember that the Forest Preserve land is to be "forever wild." This means that no standing trees may be legally cut. Use dead and downed wood only. While everyone enjoys a campfire at night, you'll find that camp cooking will be cleaner, faster, and can be done safely in more places if a small portable camper's stove is carried with you on overnight trips.

15

Winter Hiking

Winter hiking, snow shoeing, and cross-country skiing are all becoming very popular. Many of the trips included in this guidebook are excellent for these activities.

The individual must keep in mind that hiking in the winter is far different from summer hiking. Travel times will be much longer. Energy demands are greater. Clothing requirements are more strict. Tolerances for error are much less. Winter in the woods is beautiful, but do not take preparation for even an afternoon's outing lightly. Weather conditions in the Adirondacks can be as severe as those found anywhere else on this earth. Wet rains and freezing winds can be disastrous. Whiteouts can turn a short mountain climb into an overnight struggle for survival.

The novice should gain winter experience in organized groups such as the chapters of the Adirondack Mountain Club and with knowledgeable individuals. Fortunately both are readily available throughout the northeast. Do not go out alone in the winter. It is recommended, in summer or winter, to have at least four members in your group as a minimum for safety. In case of injury this permits one person to remain with the injured party, while the other two go for help.

Fire Towers

Many of the trails described in this guidebook lead up to fire towers on mountain summits. A word of caution must be issued concerning their use. The Department of Environmental Conservation is currently in a

16

transitional phase in its use of fire towers. Different means of fire protection, such as air surveillance, are being tested and many fire towers are not manned at this time. Use of unmanned fire towers is not encouraged. In some cases they are in poor condition and must be considered dangerous. The hiker is strongly urged to use good judgement and safe procedures around fire towers.

Travel Safety

The hiker is reminded that trail conditions vary through time. Rains make some areas very slippery. Spring meltwaters can wash out bridges.

While trails are generally in good repair, manpower for trail maintenance is a continuing problem. It behooves the hiker to use common sense and reasonable precautions if unusual conditions are encountered.

Trail Corrections

Trail changes are inevitable. It would be greatly appreciated if hikers would notify the Adirondack Mountain Club when such changes are found. In this way, future guidebook editions can be updated and corrected. Send such information to Adirondack Mountain Club, 174 Glen St., Glens Falls, New York 12801.

Map Update

In 1978 and 1979 much of the Adirondack High Peak region was resurveyed by the USGS, and new metric maps were developed. Please note that the following trips are now covered by the 7.5 by 15-minute metric maps listed:

Boreas Mt. . . . . Mt. Marcy (continued on Schroon Lake 15-min. quad.)
Hopkins. . . . . Elizabethtown and Keene Valley
The Brothers Trail and Loop Option . . . . Keene Valley
Balanced Rocks on Pitchoff Mt. . . . . Keene Valley
Noonmark Mt. . . . . Keene Valley, Mt. Marcy, and Elizabethtown
The Crows . . . . Lake Placid, Lewis
Ampersand Mt. . . . . Ampersand Lake
Owen and Copperas Ponds . . . . Lake Placid
Wanika Falls. . . . . Ampersand Lake
Mt. Jo. . . . . Keene Valley
Taylor Pond. . . . . Wilmington

The Adirondacks

Some particular place generally comes to mind when a person thinks about the "Adirondacks." It may be a summer camp, a favorite hiking trail, or the special view from a certain mountain top. Whatever or wherever it may be, it is almost always a relatively small geographical area with which the individual has developed intimacy. Each person creates for himself a private concept of what constitutes the "Adirondacks."

However, let's take a look at the whole of the Adirondacks for a moment. It is as large as the state of Connecticut and as varied as the people who live there. It is an Adirondacks that few people seem to know a great deal about, even though they may have gone to "their" Adirondacks for many years.

We can broadly divide the Adirondacks into two sections. The Mountain Belt consists of five parallel ranges running southwestward from Lake Champlain. They are the Luzerne Range, Kayaderosseras Range, Schroon Range, Bouquet Range, and the Adirondack Range. The second great division is the Lake Region to the west of the Mountain Belt. This comparatively flat country is covered with long chains of lakes separated by rolling forests.

Part of the vast Canadian Shield, the Adirondacks are very old. Over a billion years ago, intrusions far beneath the surface of the earth melted and forced their way from Canada into the heart of this region. Then, swelling upward like a gigantic blister, the doming process which culminated in today's high peaks slowly began.

Anorthosite rock formed under these conditions. This grey-blue plagioclase feldspar with book lenses of mica is readily found throughout this area. Away from the center, more moderate forces changed the existing rock less. Around this core, gneisses are found. The alternation of different colored bands of minerals often makes them obvious to those who are looking for them. Since these geological activities changed the original rock, the rocks are said to be metamorphic.

Most metamorphic rock is more dense than the original rock from which it formed. It has experienced so much pressure that water can no longer penetrate it. Thus the winter meltwaters must drain off the surface, rather than become subsurface groundwater.

Long Lake, Indian Lake, and Lake George are just a few examples of places where extensive breaks in the rock, called faults, have filled with water. The sharply angular turns that characterize so many Adirondack streams show where other rock breaks, called joint patterns, are followed by runoff waters. It seems that every depression forms a pond.

During its more recent geological history, the Ice Age sculptured this land. Rounding off mountain tops and filling in valleys, glaciers created still more lakes. Isolated blocks of ice sank into the ground and then melted. Kettlehole lakes, such as Heart Lake, resulted from this process. Where no drainage was possible from a depression, bogs formed. Receding glaciers frequently built a series of natural dams called moraines. Chains of lakes, so common in the Adirondacks, formed behind these moraines.

Glacial erratic, Azure Mountain

Hence, the stage upon which the dynamic drama of life in the Adirondacks is played has three principal parts. The hard platform floor keeps the waters on or near the land surface. The geological processes which made this region have provided channels through which the waters may drain off. The last Ice Age made this drainage difficult, so much water remains.

The hard metamorphic rock breaks down slowly. The soils are shallow because of this. As grades increase on mountainsides, the effects of erosion become more pronounced. Soil thickness becomes very thin. Heavy rains may saturate this soil. Landslides may then carry soil, trees, and everything else into the valleys.

It is on this thin mountain soil that man builds his trails. Newcomers frequently wonder why these trails often seem to go up stream beds. They don't realize that these "trail" streams came after man, not before him. His relentless walking has broken the soil and gravity has carried it away.

Over the years the trails become the low spots into which the surrounding waters descended. There is a lesson to be learned here. Always walk on rock where possible. Don't start that first depression that may become a stream bed in twenty years.

A trail stream

The kinds of plant life found in the Adirondacks are many. While the local environment will determine exactly which species will be found in a given area, Adirondack vegetation can be broadly grouped into five categories. They are referred to as site types. They are white pine, spruce swamp forest, mixed wood, hardwoods, and upper spruce slope sites. Characterized by a few readily identified trees, these sites tend to have specialized wildlife communities of plants and animals.

The white pine site type is generally found on sandy plains areas. From Lake Champlain to Glens Falls it predominates. White pines and other trees which have deep tap roots are most common. Mineral soils restrict what can survive there.

The spruce swamp site type is found wherever peaty or mucky soils occur in wet areas. If the swampy area has stagnant water, black spruces will be most common. If the water can flow easily, red spruce and balsam firs will be dominant.

Above the swampy zones the mixed woods begin. The term "mixed woods" refers to the fact that both softwood and hardwood trees are found growing together in the same area. Soils are better and are slightly drier. Red maple, yellow birch, and hemlocks are most common. The softwoods decrease as elevations increase. The upper limit of this site type is reached where beeches begin to be seen.

Drainage is ideal on the lower mountain slopes. This is where the hardwood site type is found. The soils are very productive here. The primary trees are sugar maples and beech. However, yellow birch, black cherry, white ash, and other trees are found in lesser numbers.

Finally, at about 2500 ft. (765 m.), the upper spruce slope site type begins. The red spruce and balsam fir again dominate. Tree size decreases as elevation increases. A timber line is reached if the mountain is high enough. The paper birch and mountain ash are the only hardwoods found in this site type, and they'll only be found at the lower limits of elevation.

Learn to identify these few trees and you'll better appreciate the forest you're traveling through on your outings. It's contagious. You'll soon be wondering why the ferns in the spruce swamp are different from those of the hardwoods. Why do the spring flowers linger longer on the trail edges than deeper in the forest? You'll begin to notice that bird species change as elevation and tree types change. Subtle but powerful biological interactions are set into motion by slight environmental variances. You will begin to notice them. Your day's hiking destination won't seem quite as important. Each step will bring new opportunities for discovery.

What might you discover? Well, it is in the Adirondacks that one of the world's great moss collections is found, clinging to the wet cliffs and ledges. You might notice the great long winding glacial ridges called eskers. Huge white pines are often found growing on them. In the acidic bogs you may discover delicate sundew plants or thick waxy pitcher plants. Trees can also tell you much. The gradual reddening of the birch bark as you gain elevation gives clues as to how far you have yet to climb. When the hardwoods blend into the red spruce and balsam fir, you'll know that you're getting along on your climb. Paper birches at high elevations are signs of past forest fires. Mixed woods tell you how long it has been since the last lumbering. Why is it that the hemlocks, so common around Lake George, are found only in wind-protected vales in the high peaks?

Everything you see in the Adirondacks has an interesting history. Varying physical factors combine to form distinctive local environments. Organisms must adapt to these environments or perish. Everything affects everything else. Remember that you also affect everything else.

Think of the whole of the Adirondacks as you seek out the charms of the special places that will become "your" Adirondacks. Take time to observe that which surrounds you. Learn the story it has to tell. It is the gift of the ages, and it began long before Man appeared to sing its praises.

Hardwood site, Snowy Mountain

Adirondak Loj, Heart Lake

The Adirondack Mountain Club

Since the Adirondack Mountain Club (ADK) was founded in 1922, it has been a spokesman for outdoor and conservation activities in New York State. Its members seek to increase citizen appreciation of nature through wholesome outing experiences and sound conservation practices. Organized into local Chapters, members can find experienced and knowledgeable persons to share almost any desired activity: Hiking, backpacking, camping, canoeing, skiing, snowshoeing, and winter mountaineering are but some of the activities carried on by the Chapters.

Members enjoy the Club Outings as well as extended trips throughout the United States and the world. Training at various skill levels is available in backpacking, canoeing, rock climbing, natural history, winter mountaineering, and wilderness leadership. Some members participate in search and rescue efforts.

Conservation activity is carried on by the Club for state-wide concerns and by the Chapters for local matters. Trail maintenance in the Adirondack High Peak Region is performed by Club volunteers and a highly skilled professional crew, hired seasonally. Some Chapters also assume trail responsibility in areas outside this region.

The Club sponsors outdoor skills instruction and educational programs which promote the appreciation and careful use of New York's wild lands. Numerous publications on outdoor activities and natural history topics are published by the Club; educational pamphlets are also available. Members receive the Club's 10-times-yearly publication, *Adirondac,* and many Chapters publish their own newsletters listing hike schedules, monthly programs, and special activities.

ADK operates two mountain lodges that serve as educational and recreational centers for both Club members and the general public. Adirondak Loj, open all year, is a rustic, historic lodge on the site of Henry VanHoevenberg's original log hotel. Located eight miles south of Lake Placid on Heart Lake, the complex is situated where many trails to the Adirondack High Peak Wilderness Region of New York State begin.

The Loj accommodations include private and bunk rooms for 46 persons. Hearty meals are served family style in the dining room. A lounge with fireplace and a small library offers a congenial atmosphere for after-dinner activities.

The campgrounds, open year round, consist of thirteen lean-tos and 37 campsites. All lean-tos and campsites are open for winter camping, but sites for trailers and campers are usually inaccessible during snow months. The High Peaks Information Center houses a large public room with educational displays, the latest backcountry information, and restrooms with hot showers. Its trading post offers last-minute camping and skiing supplies, trail snacks, and Adirondack-oriented publications.

In summer, a resident Naturalist conducts seminars and programs and maintains a small nature museum. An outdoor amphitheatre and several nature trails round out the Loj offerings. Ski rentals, guided tours, and instruction from an Adirondack guide are available in the winter.

The Club also operates Johns Brook Lodge (JBL), a simple and informal complex 3½ miles by foot travel from the trailhead near Keene Valley. JBL provides an ideal base for hiking in the Adirondack High Peak Region. The main lodge is fully staffed from late June through Labor Day, and can be used on a caretaker basis into October.

The two out-buildings, Winter Camp and Grace Camp, have simple facilities where campers may cook their own meals and sleep in snug rooms year 'round. Campers using these facilities must supply their own sleeping equipment and pack in all necessary food and supplies. There are also three lean-tos available by reservation.

Because they adjoin state land, both lodges afford unlimited mountain adventures and offer a wide choice of trails with a variety of lengths and degrees of difficulty. A large portion of the Adirondack High Peaks (4000 ft. or over) are within reach of Adirondak Loj and JBL.

Further information about ADK may be obtained by contacting the Adirondack Mountain Club, Inc., 174 Glen Street, Glens Falls, New York 12801, telephone 518/793-7737.

LAKE GEORGE AND SOUTHEAST SECTION

An hour north of Albany, the Lake George and Southeast Section of the Adirondacks is readily accessible by Interstate 87 (Adirondack Northway). Very interesting hiking and climbing opportunities, often bypassed by motorists, are available. It is a region of open rocky summits and ridges where unencumbered viewing may be enjoyed.

Where can one find a more compelling sight than Lake George surrounded by a quilt of multicolored leaves in autumn? Reds, yellows, and purples of all descriptions create a panorama of great splendor.

The Tongue Mountain Range forms a peninsula jutting out into Lake George. Its mountains are, from the north, Brown Mountain, Huckleberry Mountain, Five Mile Mountain, Fifth Peak, French Point Mountain, and First Peak. Across the lake stands Black Mountain, followed by Erebus Mountain, Buck Mountain, and numerous smaller peaks.

It must be mentioned that rattlesnakes are occasionally seen on the Tongue Mountain Range and Black Mountain. The timber rattlesnake of New York State is a relatively shy creature, however; it will wish to avoid you even more than you wish to avoid it. They are not likely to be seen along the hiking trails, though normal precautions should be taken. When climbing, take care where you put your hands on ledges. Examine the far side of the logs before stepping over them. Be observant in sunny areas, where reptiles are likely to be found. Autumn hikers will find that these cold-blooded reptiles are usually far underground by the time the leaves have turned color.

The other mountains in this section stand out by themselves. Hadley Mountain is furthest south. It is a good mountain to climb in the spring, since its rocky trail has little of the mud so common at that time of year. Pharaoh Mountain, to the north, is reached by one of the many trails that abound in the region around Paradox Lake. Crane Mountain, to the west of Warrensburg, is a delightful climb.

The Tongue Mountain Range

The Tongue Mountain Range Trail has been broken up into three separate day trips. Experienced hikers may wish to combine them for longer outings. For instance, if two cars are available, you may wish to leave one at each end of the trail and hike through to Clay Meadows from the north end. The loop from Clay Meadows to Montcalm Point via French Pt. Mountain and back to Clay Meadows from Northwest Bay is a long 12.8 m. (20.7 km.). It should not be attempted by novices. There is no easy way out should an emergency occur. For experienced hikers, however, this is a tremendously rewarding circuit.

Access to the Tongue Mountain Range is via Rte. 9N. This route may be reached from Lake George Village or by exiting Rte. 87 at Interchange 24 and then driving east to Rte. 9N. From the junction of the two roads, it is 4.7 m. (7.5 km.) further north on Rte. 9N to Clay Meadows. This is 0.2 m. (0.3 km.) beyond the boat launching site at Northwest Bay. The trailhead at the north end of the Tongue Mountain Range is another 7.3 m. (11.8 km.) north of Clay Meadows, just before the descent off Tongue Mountain begins. DEC signs mark each trailhead. There is parking available at each location.

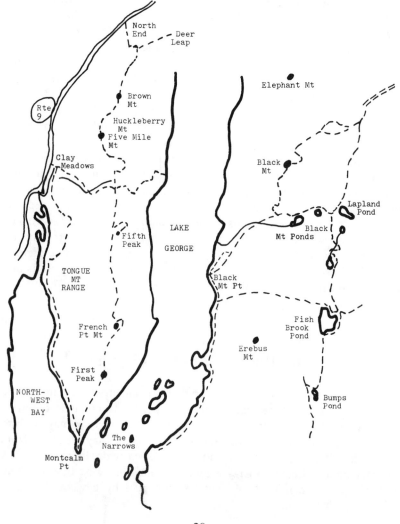

1. FIVE MILE MOUNTAIN

Round Trip Time—4 hrs. 30 min.
Round Trip Distance—7.0 m. (11.3 km.)
Elevation Change—1258 ft. (385 m.)
Summit Elevation—2258 ft. (691 m.)
Difficulty—Easy for experienced hikers,
    moderate for novices.
Map—Bolton Landing Quadrangle

This is a good trip for beginners. Open views reward the climber for much of the way. The tired tramper can turn back at any point and still feel satisfied that it was worthwhile. There is no water on this route. Take liquids with you.

Follow blue DEC markers from the trailhead. A short distance from the start, the trail makes a sharp left turn off the fire road. There is a DEC register at this location. Continuing on, the gently rising trail meets a yellow DEC marked trail at a junction at 0.65 m. (1.0 km.). The yellow trail leads straight ahead 1.0 m. (1.6 km.) to a lookout at Deer Leap.

Following the blue markers, the main trail bears right, up a slight rise. Several lookouts appear as elevation is gained. Black Ledges is reached at 1.2 m. (1.0 km.). From the rocks to the left front excellent viewing is found. Mother Bunch Islands are seen in the lake below and Black Mountain rises to the east. After leaving Black Ledges, you shortly arrive at the summit of Brown Mountain.

Proceeding onward, a careful observer may be able to see Northwest Bay through the trees to the right. Following open ledges and woods, Tongue Mountain lean-to is seen at 2.6 m. (4.2 km.). It makes a nice resting place. The lichen and flowers found growing on the open rock slopes around the lean-to are fascinating to study or to photograph. Walk on the bare rock as much as possible to protect this vegetation. From the lean-to, marvelous vistas of the Adirondack High Peaks spread out before you to the northwest.

The trail follows rock cairns and blue painted arrows over rock to the right rear of the lean-to. Easy grades lead another 0.7 m. (1.1 km.) over Huckleberry Mountain to a sign in an open spot. Only the remains of a fireplace indicate that there was once another lean-to at this location.

Finally the top of Five Mile Mountain is gained at 3.5 m. (5.7 km.). Good views of Black Mountain are obtained. The Green Mountains of Vermont are seen beyond Black Mountain to the northeast. Outstanding views can be found on the downslopes of the mountain further to the south.

If a second car has been left at Clay Meadows, it is possible to continue on to the four-way junction in the col 1.65 m. (2.7 km.) further along the trail. Then, it is another 1.95 m. (3.2 km.) to Clay Meadows. This would make a loop totaling 7.1 m. (11.5 km.). There is an 800 ft. (245 m.) drop in elevation on a steep trail from Brown Mountain to the junction.

The trail just described from the north end of Tongue Mountain to the summit of Brown Mountain is an excellent snowshoeing route.

Grasses, Tongue Mountain

Lily, Tongue Mountain

White pine needles,
Tongue Mountain

Lichen, Tongue Mountain

2. FIFTH PEAK

Round Trip Time—3 hrs. 30 min.
Round Trip Distance—5.4 m. (8.6 km.)
Elevation Change—1350 ft. (413 m.)
Summit Elevation—1770 ft. (541 m.)
Difficulty—Generally easy but steady climbing.
Map—Bolton Landing Quadrangle

Parking is found on the east side of the road, just north of Clay Meadows. From the trailhead, follow blue DEC markers on a level, and then gradually descending, trail.

As you pass through a stand of white pine, interesting ground cover can be seen. A trail junction is reached at 0.4 m. (0.6 km.). Continue straight ahead, now following red trail markers. The tote road now begins to rise at a moderately steep grade through a mixed wood forest. A cascading brook is crossed on an old bridge.

Another five minutes, and the trail becomes more rocky. Watch for where the trail makes a sharp left and then a sharp right turn. The path then levels. For a while it becomes a pleasant stroll. Gradual climbing begins again at two switchbacks. Downed branches may require that you take care to keep trail markers in view in this short section. A spring is passed on the left, as the trail swings upward to the right.

At 1.95 m. (3.2 km.), a four way junction is found. The red trail continues straight ahead, where it eventually descends to Five Mile Point on Lake George far below. The trail left goes 1.7 m. (2.7 km.) up to the summit of Five Mile Mountain.

Follow the blue trail, right, for Fifth Peak. Another 0.55 m. (0.9 km.) further on, a small sign at a trail junction indicates you must take a side trail to the left. Fifth Peak is 1500 ft. (459 m). along this side trail. A curving path leads you to a lean-to and the marvelous vantage point beyond.

What a magnificent view awaits you. Green islands, like emeralds, glitter below in the deep blue lake. From the grassy lookout, Black, Erebus, and Elephant Mountains stand out across the lake. To the south, French Mountain is prominent.

The Mohawks called the beautiful body of water you are looking at *Andia-to-roc-tee* (place where the lake contracts). Father Isaac Jogues, returning to these Indians in 1646, christened it Lac Du St. Sacrament (Lake of the Blessed Sacrament). General William Johnson gave the lake its present name, Lake George, in commemoration of King George II.

There is a delicate appearance in this region that reminds one more of the Catskills than of the high peaks of the Adirondacks. Hemlocks and white pines are found instead of the expected red spruce and balsam fir. Ground cover and open grassy slopes grace the ridges. The windswept upper reaches provide continuously changing scenes as you hike along.

3. NORTHWEST BAY TO MONTCALM POINT
Round Trip Time—4 hrs. 30 min.
Round Trip Distance—10.8 m. (17.5 km.)
Elevation Change—190 ft. (58 m.)
Difficulty—Easy; a long gradual upgrade is
found near the end of the return trip.
Map—Bolton Landing Quadrangle

This is a beautiful ramble, following an old tote road to Montcalm Point. Fully two thirds of the trip is along the shoreline of Northwest Bay.

Starting at Clay Meadows, the trail leads off to the east, following blue markers. Gradually descending, it crosses a swampy stream on a long corduroy bridge.

Keep alert for the abrupt turn to the right that the trail takes at 0.4 m. (0.6 km.). A red trail continues straight ahead where your trail swings to the right down a bank. The steady drop in elevation seems nice, but it may appear to be much longer on the return trip.

The variety of plant and animal life makes this an interesting walk. A stream and a marsh are passed. On higher, drier ground the trail parallels the inlet to Northwest Bay for some time. Birdlife abounds here and large waterbirds are commonly seen.

Lacy hemlocks cloak the shoreline. Old axe blazes mark the original route. The path follows the water's edge, occasionally climbing to avoid obstacles, but soon returning to the crystalline water. A few streams and one very attractive little waterfall beckon you to quench your thirst along the way.

At 5.0 m. (8.1 km.), a trail jct. is reached. The blue trail markers lead left and begin the climb up the ridge which meanders on for 5.3 m. (8.6 km.) to Fifth Peak lean-to and then beyond. Proceed straight ahead to the point.

Montcalm Point is named after the Marquis de Montcalm. His large military force laid siege to Ft. William Henry during the French and Indian Wars. James Fennimore Cooper's *Last of the Mohicans* made this event forever famous. Montcalm was never able to adequately explain why his forces permitted their Indian allies to massacre hundreds of surrendering men, women, and children on that grizzly morning in August, 1757.

From the point, the Narrows of Lake George are seen to the north. Across the lake is Shelving Rock. Erebus Mountain is seen to the north, on the east side of the lake. Buck Mountain rises to the right of Shelving Rock.

Narrows of Lake George

4. BUCK MOUNTAIN

Round Trip Time—4 hrs.
Round Trip Distance—6.6 m. (10.7 km.)
Elevation Change—1985 ft. (607 m.)
Difficulty—Easy for most part, moderately
**   difficult in a few places.**
Map—Bolton Landing Quadrangle

Buck Mountain offers splendid views of the Lake George Mountains and the Adirondack peaks far beyond to the north. Unique, however, is the sight sometimes seen from this bald peak, when the hiker gazes down at the water below. Dozens of small sailing craft form myriads of ever-changing patterns as their sailors exhibit their skills. On a sunny summer weekend, the spectacle is one not soon forgotten.

Access to the trailhead is best gained from the Adirondack Northway at Interchange 20. Follow Rte. 9 northward a short distance and turn right onto Rte. 149. This is the road to Whitehall. Just past a golf course on the left, turn left onto Rte. 9L. Follow this northward until you come to the right hand turn for Pilot Knob and Kattskill Bay. This is Pilot Knob Road. Follow it approximately 3.0 m. (4.9 km.) until you see the large DEC sign and parking area on the right for Buck Mountain.

The trail leaves the rear of the parking area. It follows a wide woods road. Passing occasional side trails, it crosses a creek about ten minutes along the way. Alternating grades and leveling-off spots provide rather easy walking. The mixed wood forests are very pleasant. The smell of hemlock awakens your senses.

A second stream is crossed and then a junction is reached at 1.2 m. (1.9 km.). The trail right leads 3.1 m. (5.0 km.) to Inman Pond and 2.1 m. (3.4 km.) to the Lower Hogtown parking area.

The Buck Mountain trail curves upward to the left and soon reaches a metal pipe on the right, where cool water is gushing forth. This is the last sure water on the mountain. The route gradually changes from a woods road to a path. Avoid a side trail to the right that soon appears. Yellow DEC markers soon become evident and should be followed.

The first substantial steep grade is soon surmounted, and gradual grades are again the norm. The trail curves left as a wet area is passed. A second and much longer steep grade brings you to the first lookout, on the right from which Crossett Pond is seen to the east.

The walking is now level for about ten minutes. As the grade steepens moderately, you break out on the open rock, where views to the east and south begin to appear. Following yellow painted markers ever upward, new sights quickly appear.

34

The delicate vegetation of the open rock is easily destroyed. Walk on bare rock where possible and don't stray from the trail. Protect this fragile biota.

Moving upward, the trail drops into a small rock depression and a trail junction is reached. To the right, the trail leads on another 2.5 m. (4.1 km.) to Shelving Rock. Continuing to the left front, the Buck Mountain route leads generally northwest over bare rock to a magnificent outlook, just past the high point of rock.

From here, sailboats flitter about below like water bugs. Crane Mountain is to the west. Prospect Mountain can be seen to the southeast. Across the lake to the north is the Tongue Mountain Range and Northwest Bay. Beyond them stretches the panorama of Adirondack High Peaks. Up the lake on the east shore is Erebus Mountain and Black Mountain with its tower just visible. Directly below is Pilot Knob.

As you look downward to the northwest over Little Buck Mountain toward Shelving Rock, it is easy to see why this whole open rock expanse was once called the "deer pasture."

5. BLACK MOUNTAIN LOOP

Round Trip Time—4 hrs.
Round Trip Distance—6.7 m. (10.7 km.)
Elevation Change—1200 ft. (367 m.)
Summit Elevation—2646 ft. (809 m.)
**Difficulty—Easy climbing, with occasional
        steepness.**
Map—Bolton Landing Quadrangle

"A sentinel, it seems, overlooking the whole lake and mountains round about, the first to welcome the rising sun, and at evening, glowing in the splendor of the dying day, while the valleys below are misty with the shadows of the coming night." This is how Seneca Ray Stoddard described Black Mountain in 1890 in *Lake George and Lake Champlain*. He was right. The highest mountain on the shores of Lake George, it provides an unsurpassed panorama of both the lake and the Adirondacks to the west.

Access to the trailhead is off Rte. 22, north of Whitehall. Approximately 4.5 m. (7.3 km.) north of where Rte. 22 crosses Lake Champlain is a sign for Hulett's Landing. Turn left and proceed 2.7 m. (4.4 km.) to Pike Brook Road. Turn left and travel another 0.8 m. (1.3 km.) along Pike Brook Road. As you begin to descend a hill, the large DEC sign and parking area is seen on the right. This is 3.5 m. (5.6 km.) from Rte. 22.

The trail leads up a slope a short distance to a woods road. Turn left and follow this road 0.5 m. (0.8 km.) to a trail junction just before a private home. From this point the fire tower on top of Black Mountain can be seen. The trail leaves the road to the right and skirts the private property. Do not stray off the trail at this point.

The small red DEC trail markers should be followed. A snowmobile trail, having large orange markers, winds in and out of the hiking trail. Be sure to follow the smaller trail markers.

The wide woods road you are now following continues gradually upward. A sign soon indicates a side trail left to Lapland Pond. Pass it by and continue straight forward. Not far beyond this junction the trail forks. The snowmobile trail branches up a hill to the right. The hiking trail drops down a slight grade to the left.

Soon the trail begins to climb gently again. A spring is passed on the right. A rushing brook is soon crossed. The woods road terminates and the trail becomes a footpath. Surmounting a rocky slope, it levels somewhat before winding its way up to the fire observer's cabin and fire tower.

The sight one beholds as the summit is reached will long be remembered. The Narrows of Lake George are below you. The Tongue Mountain Range stretches out along the opposite shoreline. Mt. Marcy and her court are seen in the far distance. Elephant Mountain is to the North and Erebus Mountain is to the south. The Green Mountains of Vermont are seen to the east, beyond the southern part of Lake Champlain. Note the color difference between Lake George and this section of Lake Champlain.

If one were to return by the same route, the round trip distance would be 5.0 m. (8.1 km.). The loop trail provides a much more interesting journey, however.

The trail drops off the west side of the mountain. It leads 1.3 m. (2.1 km.) to Black Mountain Pond. This trail descends rapidly with several switchbacks. Several outstanding vantage points offer excellent views of the lake below.

Near the base of the mountain a trail junction is reached. Turn left and follow yellow trailmarkers past Black Mountain Pond and then Round Pond. There is a lean-to at the first pond.

As you leave this area, the snowmobile trail is again seen, coming in from the right. Your trail leads straight on, up a small grade. Yellow markers take you onward for another twenty minutes. Keep your eyes on the markers in this section. You will reach Lapland Pond junction. You are now 2.2 m (3.6 km.) from your starting point.

Turning left, follow blue markers from this junction. The trail soon becomes a woods road again. It is generally level. Eventually you will arrive at a beautiful brook with a bridge over it. Its cooling waters provide a much appreciated respite. A slight grade brings you to the road back to the parking area. Turn right here. It is a little under a mile back to the trail origin.

6. HADLEY MOUNTAIN
Round Trip Time—3 hrs.
Round Trip Distance—4.0 m. (6.4 km.)
Elevation Change—1526 ft. (467 m.)
Summit Elevation—2675 ft. (818 m.)
Difficulty—Easy, but climbs steadily for the
    first 1.5 m. (2.4 km.).
Map—Lake Luzerne Quadrangle

Hadley Mountain provides the climber with an extremely rewarding experience. It is a good mountain to take youngsters up since the grade, though steady, is not difficult. The view will certainly make them want to continue hiking. It is also a totally enjoyable mountain to snowshoe on.

Access to the mountain is from the village of Hadley. Hadley is best reached from the east on Rte. 9N. If coming from the west, around the Great Sacandaga Lake, follow the Conklingville Road. In Hadley, turn onto Stony Creek Road. Drive north about 3 m. (4.9 km.) until you come to the marked Hadley Hill Road on the left. Proceed along the Hadley Hill Road a little over 4 m. (6.5 km.) until you come to Tower Road. There is a small sign on the right side of the road. This is the second major right-hand turn along Hadley Hill Road. This road descends a long grade for another 1.5 m. (2.4 km.) to the Hadley Mountain trailhead. It is on the left and is marked by a sign. Parking for several cars is available in the summer. In the winter, it will be necessary to squeeze your car to the side of the road so other cars will be able to pass.

The trail follows the fire observer's jeep track up the mountain. The destruction such vehicles cause is readily apparent. The top soil has been completely stripped away. However, the bare rock makes a relatively dry ascent route even in wet weather. The hiker is urged to stay on the trail, and not follow the telephone line, so that even more erosion will not occur.

The red DEC marked trail starts up through a nice hemlock stand. The steady easy to moderate grade continues for 1.5 m. (2.4 km.) until the top of West Mountain Ridge is reached. The mixed wood forest trail is interspersed with glacial boulders, small cliffs, and other features. It is an interesting walk.

Once on the ridge top, the trail turns to the right heading northwest. The last 0.5 m. (0.8 km.) is very open. Superior views make this a pleasant stroll. As the trail curves around the ridge below the fire tower, new vistas continually present themselves to the climber.

The summit is almost entirely open. It is not necessary to climb the tower. The Great Sacandaga Lake is due south. On a clear day the Helderbergs and Catskills can be seen beyond the lake. Some high peaks can be seen to the north, from the tower. Pharoah Mountain and the Green Mountains of Vermont are to the east. Spruce Mountain is to the west. It is the kind of mountain where you'll want to spend a long time on the top. Walks along the ridge to the north are quite enjoyable.

Hadley Mountain view in winter

7. CRANE MOUNTAIN

Round Trip Time—4 hrs.
Round Trip Distance—7.4 m. (12.0 km.)
Elevation Change—1154 ft. (353 m.)
Summit Elevation—3254 ft. (995 m.)
Difficulty—The middle section is quite steep,
    but most of the rest is easy.
Map—North Creek Quadrangle

This rocky summit provides some stiff climbing but is well worth it. The best way to approach the mountain is by the Wevertown—Johnsburg—Thurman Route. From Wevertown, on Rte. 28, drive 2.0 m. (3.2 km.) southwest on Rte. 8 to Johnsburg. At Johnsburg, turn south onto South Johnsburg Road and proceed 6 m. (9.6 km.) to a T intersection at Thurman. There is a small Crane Mountain sign at this intersection. Turn right onto Garnet Lake Road. Follow this road 1.5 m. (2.4 km.) to where a second, but smaller, Crane Mountain sign indicates another right hand turn. Travel this good gravel road approximately 2.0 m. (3.2 km.) until it ends at a small parking area at the trailhead. The last half mile (0.8 km.) of this road narrows considerably and more care is needed in driving.

The trailhead begins at the road end and a DEC register is seen soon after. There are two trails up the mountain from this point. A short, very steep trail leads straight ahead from the register. The trail to the left is longer, but far more interesting. It is this second route that is described here.

From the register, take the left fork along a level track. At 0.4 m. (0.6 km.), this path widens as it merges with an old abandoned woods road. Bearing right, this delightful lane leads another rolling mile (1.6 km.) to a marked intersection near the old Putnam Farm.

Turn right. Soon after this section begins, a natural bridge is crossed. On a hot day the cool breezes emanating from the stream channel's tunnel make a closer inspection of this natural phenomenon very refreshing. Beyond the bridge, one begins a gradual climb that greatly steepens as it approaches Crane Pond.

In the 0.9 m. (1.5 km.) distance from the Putnam Farm intersection to Crane Pond Outlet, the trail gains some 900 ft. (275 m.) in elevation. Views begin to open up and the rocky path requires your attention.

Turn right at Crane Pond Outlet and follow the shoreline. The summit can be seen across the water. At one time the fire observer's cabin was located at this pond's edge. Avoid the cross-over trail to the other summit trail that comes in from the right. Instead, continue around the shoreline to the north. The trail eventually swings away from the pond's perimeter path. After climbing up through the woods, you'll reach a rocky ridge in about fifteen minutes. Offering several outlooks, the open ridge trail winds southeastward to where the fire tower once stood.

From different observational locations, many points of interest can be seen. Hadley, Blue, Baldhead, and Moose mountains are seen to the south. Indian Lake, with Snowy Mountain, is off to the northwest. Crane Mountain Pond dominates the view to the west. The return trip might well include a cooling swim in this refreshing body of water.

A shorter alternate descent to the trailhead is possible by traveling a short distance eastward from the tower. If you can negotiate the nearly vertical drop on a suspended ladder at the onset, you'll find the rest of this route less rigorous. It is, however, challenging enough to keep your attention.

8. PHARAOH MOUNTAIN
Round Trip Time—4 hrs. 30 min.
Round Trip Distance—5.5 m. (8.9 km.) or 9.3 m. (15.1 km.)
Elevation Change—1257 ft. (384 m.)
Summit Elevation—2557 ft. (782 m.)
Difficulty—Easy for experienced hikers,
    challenging for novices.
Map—Paradox Lake Quadrangle

From the Adirondack Northway (Rte. 87), take Interchange 28. Follow Rte. 74 east a short distance to Rte. 9 and turn right (south). One-half mile (0.8 km.) down Rte. 9, turn left onto Alder Meadow Road. This road is about 2.0 m (3.2 km.) north of Schroon Lake Village.

Keep on this road for 2.2 m. (3.5 km.). At that point, bear left at the fork in the road. Travel another 1.4 m. (2.2 km.) to a parking area at the end of the road. The road is open to the parking area year round. It is a 9.3 m. (15.1 km.) round trip to the summit of Pharaoh Mountain from this point.

Crane Pond Road leads out of the right side of this parking area. It is presently maintained by the town highway department and is in better condition than in former years. When the 1986 revision of the State Land

Master Plan is put into effect, the Crane Pond Primitive Corridor is to be designated as a Wilderness Area. The Crane Pond Road will then be closed to motorized vehicles. At 1.9 m. (3.0 km.), the road terminates at the large Crane Pond parking area.

The trailhead is at the end of the parking area, where a register is located. Heading southwest from the register, over a large flat boulder, follow red markers. The outlet of Crane Pond is immediately crossed on a log bridge. The wide trail proceeds over rolling terrain. The mixed woods of hemlock, birch, and beech are particularly beautiful in autumn.

At 0.7 m. (1.1 km.), a trail junction is reached. The Pharaoh Mountain trail makes a sharp right and then a sharp left. Climbing a short rise, Glidden Marsh is seen below to the left. This is one of several trout stocked waters in this region.

A series of gradual rises indicates that you have reached the lower slopes of the mountain. From this point onward, the grades become both progressively steeper and longer.

When stopping to rest, look at the rock type of this mountain. It is basically a metamorphic gneiss formed from the original granite of this area. Note the alternating bands of light and dark colored minerals in the rock. There is great variation throughout the mountain. Each stop brings an interesting variety for those who seek them out. They give clues to what was happening in this area many millions of years ago. The reddish mineral is garnet.

The course of the former telephone line to the tower crosses the trail in several places. Follow the marked trail. It is safer. As you reach the upper third of the mountain, you'll notice the route is mostly over bare rock. When the first good open view, to the west, appears at a rocky shelf to the right, you'll know you are close to the top. One last steep climb, through a grassy area, will bring you to the fire observer's cabin and tower. The tower is currently being used, but how long it will remain open in the future is not known.

The clear rocky summit is a good place for a leisurely lunch. In season you can top it off with the blueberries that appear here. At least three bench markers and one Verplanck Colvin survey marker can be located near the fire tower. Colvin was responsible for the early surveys of the Adirondacks. His enthusiasm and wisdom played a major part in the establishment of the Adirondack State Park. Survey control points on Pharaoh Mountain were used as early as 1878.

Schroon Lake is seen to the west with Spectacle Pond, Desolate Brook, and other smaller bodies of water somewhat closer. A short walk to the southwest brings you to another vantage point from which Pharaoh Lake is seen at the base of the mountain. Treadway Mountain is to the east.

This is an excellent area for snowshoeing and skiing in the winter time.

T-Lake Falls

INDIAN LAKE AND SOUTH SECTION

This section might be called the forgotten part of the Adirondacks. Though few mountains of any great size can be found, good views can be had from those that exist. It is generally a region of rolling forest, small lakes, and quiet marshes. There is a difference here. You can be alone. In fact, on a few trails in this area you might be surprised to meet someone.

This is the land of Nick Stoner and French Louie, legendary woodsmen of yesteryear. Coyotes still abound and first time campers have been known to sit bolt upright in their sleeping bags when a loon screamed in the night.

It is good snowshoeing country. Cross-country skiers all have their favorite spots. Hunters come in season, but for the most part the hiker seeking solitude can find it.

The trips described here are easily reached by car. Rtes. 8, 10 and 30 provide access into this section.

9. WAKELY MOUNTAIN
Round Trip Time—4 hrs.
Round Trip Distance—6.0 m. (9.7 km.)
Elevation Change—1635 ft. (500 m.)
Summit Elevation—3744 ft. (1145 m.)
Difficulty—First two-thirds is easy; the last third is steep and steady.
Maps—Indian Lake and West Canada Lakes Quadrangles

The Wakely Mountain trail is a relatively flat walk on a tote road for two-thirds of its distance. The last third, however, lets you know there is a mountain. In 0.8 m. (1.3 km.) it shoots up 1200 ft. (367 m.). The view from the fire tower is outstanding. All points of the compass offer good views.

Access to the mountain is from Indian Lake village. Drive west 2.2 m. (3.6 km.) on Rte. 30. At Cedar River Cemetery, turn left onto Cedar River Road. Proceed on this road for 13.8 m. (22.4 km.). A sign and tote road on the right mark the trailhead at this point. This is not a good road on which to drive, but one can park off it at the trailhead.

Better parking is found if you travel another 0.3 m. (0.5 km.) down Cedar River Road to Cedar River Station. This is the east end of the

Moose River Recreation Area at Wakely Dam. It is a good place to park or to camp out. A cool swim, some fishing, or canoeing may be added to your hiking agenda here.

The first part of the hiking trail is unexciting. It travels through a sparse woods along a tote road. At 0.7 m. (1.0 km.) the remains of an old logging camp are passed on the left, below the road bank. A road is soon seen to the right and a stream is crossed on a wooden bridge. The route follows the stream for a short distance and then veers away. A junction marked with a Wakely Mountain sign is reached at 1.9 m. (3.1 km.). The trail has gained only about 435 ft. (133 m.) elevation at this point.

The fire observer often leaves water jugs here. The water is a most welcome treat, for the remainder of the trail is steep. From this point, very steady climbing begins on the unusually well-cared-for route.

A survey marker is seen on a rock at 2.5 m. (4.1 km.). A short distance further on you can see the fire tower above you to the right front. Not long after, a side trail to a helicopter pad is passed on the right. Then you arrive at the tower.

The viewing from the ground is restricted to the southeast. However, the fire tower provides a 360 degree vista that is very fine. Snowy Mountain is to the southeast. Blue Mountain is to the north. The lake country opens to the west.

10. SNOWY MOUNTAIN
Round Trip Time—5 hrs.
Round Trip Distance—7.5 m. (12.2 km.)
Elevation Change—2105 ft. (644 m.)
Summit Elevation—3899 ft. (1192 m.)
Difficulty—Challenging. Long hike, steep
      much of the way, fatiguing if not in good condition.
Map—Indian Lake Quadrangle

Through a joint venture with the DEC and town of Indian Lake, the Adirondack Mountain Club's trail crew greatly improved the condition of the Snowy Mountain Trail in the summer of 1987.

Snowy Mountain just misses being in the 4000-ft. (1233 m.) class by a few feet. The vertical climb is actually greater than many of the 46'er peaks, since the base is at a lower elevation.

The mountain is located on the west side of Indian Lake along Rte. 30. It is 6.5 m. (10.5 km.) south of Indian Lake village and 4.7 m. (7.6 km.) north of Lewey Lake Outlet and the boat launching site. Along the west side of the road, the trailhead for Snowy Mountain climbs a bank. A large paved area is available for parking several cars on the opposite side of the highway.

The trail heads westward up Beaver Brook Valley, following red markers. Generally flat or rolling, it crosses several small streams. Finally, after being within hearing of Beaver Brook down to the right for some time, the path leads below to the rock-bordered stream and crosses it at 1.2 m. (1.9 km.).

A steep climb for a short distance moves you off the valley floor. From this point on, however, the previously closed-in trail opens up and is more pleasant. An extremely large downed maple blocks the path near the top of the moderating grade. You may have noticed that the largest trees are sugar maples and old spruces. Beaver Brook is again crossed at 1.9 m. (3.1 km.) and young spruces are seen, beginning to emerge beneath the branches of the older trees. This is the sign of a climax forest.

Occasional hunting trails branch off, but the main trail is obvious. The route crosses from the right bank of the brook to the left bank. At 2.5 m. (4.1 km.) a tributary is crossed and you begin a long steady climb up the mountain. The soil thins and is drier. As a result, the trees now become much smaller in diameter.

Gradually the trail becomes rockier. A good lookout to the rear is found at 3.2 m. (5.2 km.). The reconditioned trail is extremely steep for the remainder of the way to the summit. The observer's cabin is reached at 3.8 m. (6.2 km.). A large cliff edge provides a fine view eastward to Indian Lake and beyond. This makes a good place for a lunch break. There is a small spring at wood's edge, near the place where the trail

45

continues to the tower, but its quality varies since the fire observer is no longer here to maintain it.

The summit is only 500 ft. (153 m.) up a gentle grade to the southwest. Unfortunately, the tower is no longer open for viewing. A trail southeast of the tower leads to an unusual lookout point where cliffs drop off several hundred feet. Another side trail takes you 50 yds. (46 m.) west of the spring to a lookout where Buell and Panther mountains can be seen. The vista down to the ponds along Squaw Brook from this place is exquisite. From the fire observer's cabin, it is possible to see Mount Marcy and the High Peaks to the north.

11. ECHO CLIFFS AT PANTHER MOUNTAIN
Round Trip Time—1 hr. 30 min.
Round Trip Distance—1.7 m. (2.7 km.)
Elevation Change—725 ft. (212 m.)
Summit Elevation—2425 ft. (742 m.)
Difficulty—Easy, with some steepness near terminus.
Map—Piseco Lake Quadrangle

Echo Cliffs, at Panther Mountain, offers a nice little climb and a surprisingly good view of Piseco Lake and areas to the east.

Access to the trailhead is from the West Shore Road along Piseco Lake. West Shore Road is off Rte. 8, 2.9 m. (4.7 km.) south of where Rte. 8 meets Rte. 10. Drive along West Shore Road 2.6 m. (4.2 km.) from Rte. 8. At this point, a small DEC sign marks the trailhead. There is parking on the opposite side of the road.

The trailhead sign indicates an ascent of 1048 ft. (320 m.). This is the vertical distance to the summit, not to Echo Cliffs. Following blue DEC markers, the trail leads through a mature maple-beech forest.

Varying grades provide relatively easy walking for the first 0.6 m. (1.0 km.), until a large boulder is reached. At this point, the way becomes more rocky and consistently steeper. Five minutes later, a large rock outcrop is passed. Soon after, the trail becomes rather steep for the short remaining distance to Echo Cliffs. Red spruce are now present, giving evidence of higher elevation.

The splendid view is to the southeast. Higgins Bay and Spy Lake are seen to the left front. Beyond Spy Lake, Three Sisters Mountains are seen. To the left is the huge bulk of Hamilton Mountain. A small portion of Oxbow Lake can be seen to the northeast. To the right front, the long narrow curved body of water beyond Piseco Lake is Big Bay.

Panther Mountain got its name, back in time, when $20 was paid for a "painter" pelt and $10 for a "whelp." There is currently some interest in trying to reestablish this needed predator again inside the Adirondack Park. By culling the old and sick, this native cat might strengthen the deer population in this region.

View from Echo Cliffs, Piseco Lake

12. T-LAKE

Round Trip Time — 4 hrs. 30 min.
Round Trip Distance — 7.3 m. (11.8 km.)
Elevation Change — 764 ft. (234 m)
Difficulty — Considerably more rugged than the
bare statistics would indicate; a long hike.
Map — Piseco Lake Quadrangle

The hike into T-Lake makes a good day's ramble. It can be lengthened by continuing on to T-Lake Falls or by doing a semi-bushwhack trip up T-Lake Mountain. However, for the normal day hike, T-Lake makes a reasonable objective.

Access is from the West Shore Road on Piseco Lake. The trailhead is a short distance south of the entrance to Poplar Point Public Campsite. The trailhead is 4.0 m. (6.5 km.) from the junction of Piseco Road and Rte. 8. This is 1.7 m. (2.8 km.) south of the DEC Northville-Placid sign post in the village of Piseco. Poplar Point Public Campsite makes a good place to leave the car, enjoy a swim after the hike, and perhaps have a picnic supper.

The trail follows red DEC markers up a moderately steep grade. It soon eases somewhat but continues on steadily up the shoulders of Piseco and Stacy Mountains. At the upper end of this climb two level sections provide respite. Both pass through cols having rocky outcrops. The ferns in the small vlei at the height of land make the second level section especially attractive.

At 1.3 m. (2.1 km.) you begin to descend. The moderate drop soon steepens. Much of your hard earned elevation is quickly lost. Various branches of Millers Creek are crossed. Most are dry. The terrain becomes up and down, and you soon begin the moderate grade up the east shoulder of T-Lake Mountain.

A rocky outcrop on the left draws your attention just before you make an abrupt turn to the left. Now you begin climbing at a moderately steep grade. A few moments later, at 2.6 m. (4.2 km.), the junction with the old trail is reached. It comes in from the right. *Be sure not to take it on your return.*

Bearing left, you continue up the curving grade; 0.1 m. (0.2 km.) beyond this point is the branch to the left for T-Lake Mountain. This once popular mountain no longer has a fire tower. Hence, the wooded summit does not offer as fine a view as it once did.

Formerly, the red trail continued on up the mountain to the summit while blue markers pointed the way to T-Lake. This change in marker color is the only good way to determine where the old trail up the mountain begins, since no signs are found at this point today. Two small boulders on the left may give enough clue for you to find this trail, which must be considered a semi-bushwhack.

From the junction, follow the blue markers along a nearly level path. You soon catch glimpses of T-Lake, down through the trees to your right. Before you realize it, you are in front of the T-Lake lean-to. The pretty lake is down the bank a short distance.

From here you may wish to continue on another 1.8 m. (2.9 km.) to T-Lake Falls. The way is extremely nice. Reputed to be among the highest waterfalls in the Adirondacks, it is often dry in the summer. The trail comes out on the top of the falls. A cable must be used to descend the far side of the waterway to the pool below. At least two people have been killed on these falls, so care is imperative.

Perhaps a respite at the lean-to should be taken before making any decisions about going on to the falls. These trails have been tramped since the 1860's and they won't mind waiting a few moments for you to make up your mind.

13. WILCOX LAKE WALK

Round Trip Time — 5 hrs. 30 mins.
Round Trip Distance — 9.6 m. (15.6 km)
Elevation Change — 480 ft. (147 m.)
Difficulty — East walking, but a long trip.
Map — Harrisburg Quadrangle

The hike from Brownell's Camp to Wilcox Lake is a woodland ramble at its very best. It follows an old tote road through a magnificent mixed wood forest. Over half of the trip is along East Stony Creek.

Access to the trail is off Rte. 30, above the Great Sacandaga Lake, on the southern edge of the hamlet of Hope. Three & two-tenths m. (5.2 km.) north of the Benson Section signpost for the Northville-Placid Trail, turn right on Creek Road. There is a family cemetery plot at this intersection.

Proceed along Creek Road for 2.8 m. (4.5 km.) until a Y-intersection with DEC signs is reached. Turn left onto Mud Creek Road. At its midpoint it will become a dirt road. Proceed along this road 4.9 m. (7.9 km.) to a DEC signpost at the trailhead, along East Stony Creek. Park off the road as much as possible. Do not proceed onto the Brownell Camp property, which is private.

Following blue DEC markers, Tenant Creek is crossed on a good wooden bridge in about ten minutes. The trail is an old logging route through a pretty mixed wood forest. After about a mile of walking, you return to the banks of East Stony Creek.

Turning right, the woods road parallels the stream going upstream for close to 3 m. (9.9 km.). In the spring the water is high and fast moving. Its rocks, sparkling reflections, and ever changing scenes make it fascinating. In season many flowers are found along the stream banks.

Occasional tributaries are crossed. At one point, the old trail rises far up the bank until it is a considerable distance to the shimmering water below. Some time later you begin the descent to the bridge over Dayton Creek.

Just beyond Dayton Creek, be sure to take the left fork, where the tote road splits. Paralleling the stream, you reach the metal suspension bridge that crosses East Stony Creek. It is 4.4 m. (7.1 km.) straight ahead to Harrisburg Lake.

Turning left, cross the suspension bridge and begin the last 0.7 m. (1.1 km.) climb over the low shoulder of Wilcox Mountain to Wilcox Lake. Follow the large yellow snowmobile trail markers carefully in this short section. Switchbacks take you up the steady but moderate slope.

Some blowdown is passed through near the top of the grade, where a T junction is found. The left turn would take you 4.5 m. (7.3 km.) to Willis Lake.

Turn right for the last 0.2 m. (0.3 km.) down the slope to Wilcox Lake. You soon come to the jeep trail, which enters from the right. Continue straight ahead to the DEC register found at the lake's edge.

The lake is good sized and has good fishing. As you look around this handsome lake, consider that it cost "tenderfeet" $9.00 a week to stay at the Brownell Camp's woods hotel back in 1917. They came by smoky train and dusty stagecoach to spend a season in these climes. You'll probably be home in a nice soft bed tonight, having made the return drive in a few hours. Times were different, then, but not necessarily better.

14. CATHEAD MOUNTAIN
Round Trip Time—3 hrs.
Round Trip Distance—2.5 m. (4.1 km.)
Elevation Change—1273 ft. (389 m.)
Summit Elevation—2427 ft. (442 m.)
Difficulty—A short moderate climb of steady
grade, steep near the end.
Map—Lake Pleasant Quadrangle

Cathead Mountain makes a nice short afternoon's jaunt. Its tower was still manned in 1985. The mountain has been lumbered since at least 1860, when Willard Wright built a lumber mill on its lower slopes. There is yet evidence of the wood cutter, but the mountain is an enjoyable climb, generally unaffected by the sawman.

Access to the trailhead is off Rte. 30 in the village of Benson, a few miles above the Great Sacandaga Lake. Turn left towards Benson at the DEC Benson Section sign for the Northville-Placid Trail. Proceed up the long hill 2.8 m. (4.5 km.) to the right-hand turn at North Road. The town hall is at this corner, as is a small DEC sign pointing in the direction of Cathead Mountain. North Road dead-ends at the trailhead, 1.2 m. (1.9 km.) further on. Park on the right, so as not to block the private entrance that is on the left.

The red marked DEC trail follows a dirt road for a short distance and then branches off to the left. A small sign is at this junction.

The gradually rising trail is rather pleasant. About halfway up the mountain the way becomes considerably steeper and very rocky.

A few hundred feet below the summit the fire observer's cabin is reached. From this point one climbs steeply up the bare rock to the fire tower.

It is not necessary to climb the tower in order to gain a good view. To the southeast is the Great Sacandaga Lake. It is in that direction that the best views are found. Groff Mountain dominates to the north. Wallace and Three Ponds Mountains are around to the west. All in all, the bare rock of the broad summit provides a most interest setting for the hiker.

15. SAWYER MOUNTAIN
Round Trip Time — 2 hrs.
Round Trip Distance — 2.3 m. (3.7 km.)
Elevation Change — 650 ft. (199 m)
Summit Elevation — 2610 ft. (798 m.)
Difficulty — Easy.
Map — Blue Mountain Quadrangle

Sawyer Mountain is an easy climb. A new trail leads up through a mature forest of maple and beech to the lookout, just past the summit. For such a short climb, the view is very good.

Access to the trailhead is off Rte. 28, between the villages of Indian Lake and Blue Mountain Lake. It is on the west side of the road, 2.6 m. (4.2 km.) north of the bridge across the Cedar River. This is about 6.0 m. (9.7 km.) from Blue Mountain Lake village. The well-marked trailhead has excellent parking facilities.

The trail follows yellow DEC trail markers up rolling grades from the road, leveling off after a few minutes. Then, a moderately steep grade takes you over a small shoulder of a ridge and down again. Red paint blazes are mixed with occasional trail markers for the rest of the route. Climbing becomes generally moderate for the next half hour.

The pleasant trail passes to the left of a large boulder at 0.9 m. (1.5 km.). The path then levels for a short while. A lookout to the east is reached. The bare rock slope is rather steep and is biased down to the left. Immediately after starting out on the rock, the trail cuts to the right, reentering the woods. Walking is much safer there. The trail returns to the open, further upslope, where good views are found.

Trees become more widely spaced as you approach the wooded summit. The trail goes on another 270 ft. (83 m.) past the summit to an excellent lookout.

Below to your left front is Sprague Pond. Beyond it, Blue Ridge extends for several miles. In the valley to your right is a beautiful vlei. Looking due west, between the vlei and the pond, thin Stephens Pond is seen high up on the ridge. The Northville-Placid Trail skirts this pond as it winds 132 m. (214 km.) through the Adirondacks. In the far distance, Blue Mountain boldly stands out on the horizon.

THE EAGLE BAY AND
BLUE MOUNTAIN SECTION

The Eagle Bay and Blue Mountain Section is in the Lake Region of the Adirondacks. The terrain is relatively flat and is more suited to sustaining the wear and tear of the hiker's boots. Though many trails are heavily used, they retain a freshness and primitive quality that is amazing.

There is something special about this region. It takes hold of you and won't let go. Alvah Dunning, the hermit, was living in the Blue Mountain Lake area in the middle 1800's. Encroaching summer vacationers forced him on to Raquette Lake and, still later, to Eighth Lake. When guideboats became too frequent there, he really became upset. He lit out for the Rocky Mountains for peace and quiet. He was back within a year. These lakes had cast their spell over him and he could not stay away.

The lake country mountains are generally not big. You can take your time climbing them and really observe your surroundings. Yet, since the whole region is so flat, excellent views are gained from the summits of these peaks. Rtes. 28 and 30 lead into this region.

16. RONDAXE (BALD) MOUNTAIN
Round Trip Time — 1 hr. 30 min.
Round Trip Distance — 2.0 m. (3.2 km.)
Elevation Change — 400 ft. (122 m.)
Summit Elevation — 2350 ft. (719 m.)
Difficulty — Easy, with only one minor steep spot.
Map — Old Forge Quadrangle

The hardest thing about this mountain is figuring out what to call it. At first, it was just Pond Mountain. For awhile it became Foster's Observatory in honor of Nat Foster, the trapper. He said he liked to go there to get away from the Indians. After the Civil War, there was a movement by some summer residents to call it Mont. St. Louis. Now, almost everyone calls it Bald Mountain, except for the state officials. To avoid confusing it with another fire tower mountain having the same name, the Conservation Department opted to call it Rondaxe Mountain. Why Rondaxe? Named after a nearby lake, it is the phonetic corruption of the last two syllables of Adirondacks.

On any account, it's probably the most often climbed mountain inside the state park. For sheer fun and ease of climbing, it can't be beat. The summit view is superb.

Access to the trailhead is on Rondaxe Road, off Rte. 28, between Eagle Bay and Old Forge. If coming from Old Forge, Rondaxe Road is a short distance beyond the Bald Mountain Restaurant, where another trail up the mountain begins. Turning west on Rondaxe Road, drive 0.2 m. (0.3 km.) to where there is a large parking area on the left side of the road.

A large wooden map of the area and a DEC register mark the trailhead. Follow red markers. The first five minutes of walking take you through a hardwood forest on an essentially level trail.

At this point, the only steep climbing begins. Leading up bare rocks and over tree roots, this short stretch soon moderates. The first lookout is at 0.3 m. (0.5 km.).

Beyond here the climb continuously provides ever widening views of the Fulton Chain to the east. The ease of climbing combined with frequent looks at the scenery bring you to the summit almost before you are expecting it.

The trail follows a hogback ridge. Its spine tapers until, at the last, you feel that you are walking up the vertebrae of some great extinct dinosaur.

The rain shelter and fire tower are seen after about thirty minutes of hiking. Below you, to the east, large Fourth Lake meets your gaze. As your eyes swing to the right, Fourth Lake constricts to a narrow channel and becomes Third Lake. Second and First Lakes are seen further to the right. Beyond First Lake is Little Moose Lake. Turning back to the far end of Fourth Lake to the left, Blue Mountain looms above the distant horizon, twenty-eight miles away. Over fifty-six miles off, Mt. Marcy can be seen on a clear day in line with the extreme left margin of Fourth Lake. Algonquin is to the left.

Closer in, Black Bear Mountain is seen just past the end of Fourth Lake. Seventh Lake is to its right. Over the broad part of Fourth Lake, Wakely Mountain is seen in the distance.

17. CORK MOUNTAIN
Round Trip Time—2 hrs. 30 min.
Round Trip Distance—3.2 m. (5.2 km.)
Elevation Change—470 ft. (144 m.)
Summit Elevation—2285 ft. (699 m.)
**Difficulty—Easy to Carry Pond; moderately
    strenuous to summit.**
Map—Old Forge and Big Moose Quadrangles

The Cork Mountain trail is hiked not so much for the view from the summit but for the trail itself. The route is much more a primitive woods path than a broad tote road. It has a certain primeval quality. The closeness of the tree growth, the suddenness with which ponds are reached, and the variation in terrain all combine to make a most interesting trip.

Access to the trailhead is from the same parking area that is used for the Rondaxe Mountain climb. The two trips can easily be combined in one outing. About halfway between Eagle Bay and Old Forge, turn west onto Rondaxe Road. A DEC signpost at this turn indicates the direction of the parking area. Two-tenths of a mile (0.3 km.) down Rondaxe Road, the parking area is on the left side of the road. The Cork Mountain trailhead is on the opposite side of the road.

Five minutes after beginning to follow blue DEC trail markers, you descend a grade to a junction. Fly Pond is down to the left, visible through the trees. It is worth the brief side excursion to visit it.

The main trail bears right from the junction. It rather significantly winds through the woods, seeming to seek out rock outcrops that can be tramped over. Again you find yourself descending, this time to the edge of Carry Pond. This body of water is much larger than Fly Pond. Turning left, you skirt the shoreline for about ten minutes. A large beaver house can be seen (1978) as the end of the pond is reached.

Very soon thereafter, you come to the old Raquette Lake Railroad bed, at 0.7 m. (1.1 km.). A large wooden placard tells you about this railroad, which was built in 1899.

Having walked for about thirty minutes, you turn right and travel a short distance past the end of Carry Pond to a sign pointing left to Mountain Pond. Following this path, a minor wet area is passed just before you start the ascent.

For the next half hour, the trail progressively steepens. Numerous switchbacks take you up to a junction in a col. Here the blue trail leaves you, dropping down the far side of the ridge to Mountain Pond. You should follow red DEC markers straight up the mountain. In ten minutes, this very steep path brings you to the summit. Two signs point the way to lookouts.

To the northeast, the unusually green Mountain Pond is seen below. A small part of Lake Rondaxe is to the north. In the west is Bottle Mountain.

An interesting extension of this trip can be made if a second vehicle is available at the end of the trail. Dropping down to Mountain Pond, the blue trail continues along an open ridge another 2.8 m (4.5 km.). There it joins the Bub and Sis Ponds Trail. Going to the right, a twenty-minute walk would bring you out on Rte. 28 near Becker's Resort Hotel.

18. WINDFALL POND WALK AND LOOP OPTION
Round Trip Time—1 hr. and 30 min.
Round Trip Distance—2.2 m. (3.6 km.)
Elevation Change—180 ft. (55 m.)
Difficulty—Easy.
Map—Big Moose Quadrangle

The Windfall Pond Trail makes a nice little afternoon hike. It can be extended to a full day's outing if desired. The trail basically parallels the pond's outlet creek. Sometimes high above, sometimes right alongside, it is a pretty path that takes you along the brookside up to the pond.

Access to the trailhead is the large DEC parking area on the Big Moose Road from Eagle Bay. This parking area is on the northeast side of the road 3.3 m. (5.3 km.) from Eagle Bay and 0.6 m. (1.0 km.) south of Higsby Road.

Starting at the DEC register, follow yellow trail markers along an open level path. After a few moments, you cross a creek on a wooden bridge. Entering the woods, the narrow trail returns to the stream at 0.7 m. (1.1 km.). It follows the brook much of the rest of the way to Windfall Pond.

It soon climbs a grade far above the water, only to return to it a short time later. To the right of the bridge which crosses the stream is an interesting rock cleft through which water cascades in times of runoff.

Turning left across the bridge, the trail parallels the stream. The flow widens to form a vlei in places. At 0.9 m. (1.5 km.) the outlets of Queer Lake and Windfall Pond meet at a swampy area called Beaver Meadow. Here, signs point to the right for both Queer Lake and Windfall Pond.

Following the brook upward another few minutes brings you to Windfall Pond. This pretty little body of water is inundated with white lilies. The purple spikes of pickerel weed brighten the shorelines. Driftwood has collected at the fetch end of the pond.

A full day's outing can be had by going on from the trail junction at Windfall Pond. Following the yellow trail to the left for another 1.6 m. (2.6 km.) will bring you to Queer Lake after joining the red Cascade Pond trail near the lake. After seeing Queer Lake, backtrack on the red trail and follow it past Chain Ponds toward Cascade Lake for 1.4 m. (2.3 km.) to where it meets the blue trail back to Windfall Pond. Turning right, it is another 1.2 m. (1.9 km.) along the blue trail back to Windfall Pond. This would make a total day's walk from the trailhead and return of about 6.5 m. (10.5 km.).

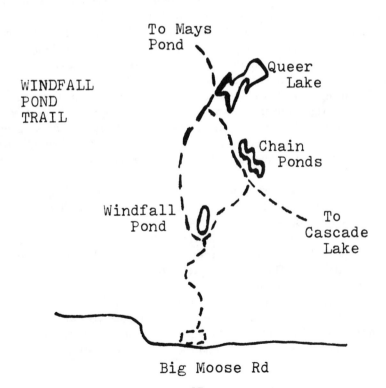

To Mays Pond

Queer Lake

WINDFALL POND TRAIL

Chain Ponds

Windfall Pond

To Cascade Lake

Big Moose Rd

19. BLACK BEAR MOUNTAIN

Round Trip Time—3 hrs.
Round Trip Distance—4.4 m. (7.2 km.)
Elevation Change—542 ft. (181 m.)
Summit Elevation—2448 ft. (749 m.)
Difficulty—Easy, with one steep section.
Map—Big Moose Quadrangle

Black Bear Mountain is an attractive peak. The first part of the trail runs over the old Uncas Road, built by J. Pierpont Morgan. He and the other elite rode over it to his camp on Mohegan Lake in a coach drawn by six plumed horses. The mountain burned over once, leaving it barren on top. Slowly recovering, much of its summit is a fascinating collection of lichen, blueberries, and mountain ash. Views in all directions are excellent.

Access to the trailhead is on Brown's Tract Pond Road, off Rte. 28, in Eagle Bay. Turn north from Rte. 28 at the DEC sign for Brown's Tract Ponds Public Campsite. This road bears left almost immediately and becomes a hard packed dirt road. The trailhead is 2.9 m. (4.7 km.) down this road on the right side. Here, a sign indicates it is 3.5 m. (5.7 km.) to Eighth Lake Public Campsite. There is parking for several cars.

The trail initially follows the Uncas Road, which is now a grassy lane. A short way along this route a cable stretches across the trail. Long, very moderate grades make progress easy. As you near the bottom of one of these grades, at 0.8 m. (1.3 km.), a sign is seen on a birch tree. It points to a side trail at the right. The summit is 1.4 m. (2.3 km.) in that direction.

Turning right, you drop down a moderately steep grade. The otherwise excellent trail has grown in some at this point but soon widens again. Crossing a brook at the bottom of the grade, you proceed along an easy trail. You again drop down a grade and cross another creek at 1.2 m. (2.0 km.).

As you climb a short, moderately steep grade, a ski trail sign will be passed on the left. Avoid this turn. Continue straight ahead where you will follow yellow nordic ski trail markers for the rest of the way.

Avoid an unmarked trail to the right a few minutes later, just before reaching a marked junction. The trail to the summit follows the expert ski trail straight ahead. The regular nordic ski trail branches right, running for another 3.0 m. (4.9 km.) to Rte. 28.

The next section of trail is much steeper than anything else to this point. Winding up through the trees, there is a branch off to a lookout at the left. You can walk the rim of the mountain for a short distance before returning to the main trail. Beyond the lookout, the path moderates. It breaks the tree line, covering the last 0.2 m. (0.3 km.) on open rock. Rock cairns guide you where the yellow markers aren't posted. In this section be sure you see the next cairn or marker before leaving the one you've just passed.

The summit is spectacular both for its unusual lichen vegetation and its view. The main vista is to the southeast. There, Seventh Lake stands out, with large Goff Island at its center. Beyond, Fawn Lake Mountain is seen, with Limekiln Lake to its right. Behind you to the north, Cascade Ridge extends toward Raquette Lake. Blue painted arrows take you a short distance westward over the rocks to another good vantage point. There, Fourth Lake is seen. Plan on spending a long time on this most interesting summit.

The trail, and especially the summit section, would appear much more suited for snowshoeing than for skiing. In fact, the trip in over the ski trail from Rte. 28 to the summit would make a nice 6 m. (9.7 km.) round trip. This ski trail begins on Rte. 28, 0.9 m. (1.5 km.) east of Brown's Tract Pond Road and is marked by a small sign. The route along Uncas Road is a snowmobile trail in the winter and probably isn't plowed from Rte. 28.

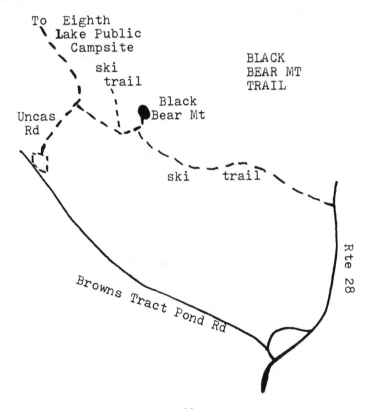

20. BLUE MOUNTAIN

Round Trip Time—3 hrs.
Round Trip Distance—4.1 m. (6.6 km.)
Elevation Change—1579 ft. (483 m.)
Summit Elevation—3759 ft. (1150 m.)
**Difficulty—Moderately difficult; middle section
   is steep.**
Map—Blue Mountain Quadrangle

Called *To-war-loon-da* by the Indians, this mountain is truly a "Hill of Storms." Its great bulk stands above the surrounding territory like a giant sentinel. In the days of Verplanck Colvin, gunpowder was set off at this summit each evening precisely at nine o'clock to help synchronize the work of his survey crews.

Trailhead access is located on the edge of Blue Mountain Lake village just north of the Adirondack Museum. From the junction of Rtes. 28 and 30, this is 1.3 m. (2.1 km.) up the hill along Rte. 30. You'll find a large parking area on the east side of the road.

Trails for Tirrell Pond and Blue Mountain both begin here. Take the red-marked trail to the right along a nearly level woods road. There is a slight increase in grade just before the route becomes a footpath and enters the woods.

Easy grades alternate with level terrain to provide pleasant walking for the next 15 minutes. You then reach a stream crossing. More challenging climbing is found beyond this point.

The way becomes increasingly rocky, until you are climbing over solid sheets of bare rock through the forest. It is unusual and comfortable on the feet. The trail becomes very steep for awhile.

The change is most welcome, however, when the trail again levels at 1.5 m. (2.4 km.). Still on bare rock, the path takes you through a pretty coniferous forest for the last 0.6 m. (1.0 km.) to the summit.

While good views are possible from the ground, the fire tower provides magnificent sightings. To the west Blue Mountain Lake is at the foot of the mountain. To its left are Eagle Lake and then Utowana Lake. Beyond the ridges Raquette Lake can be seen. To the north Minnow Pond, Mud Pond, South Pond, and finally part of Long Lake can be traced. In a northeastward direction, Tirrell Mountain, with its beautiful sandy Tirrell Pond, is below you. Just to the left and beyond is Tongue Mountain. Algonquin is in line with Tongue Mountain, another twenty-five miles (40.5 km.) in the distance. To the right of Algonquin the gap of

Avalanche Pass and then Mt. Colden can be seen. Somewhat further to the left is Ampersand Mountain, seen between Seward and the much closer Kempshall Mountain on Long Lake.

21. CASCADE POND
Round Trip Time — 3 hrs.
Round Trip Distance — 5.6 m. (9.1 km.)
Elevation Change — 361 ft. (110 m.)
Difficulty — Easy.
Map — Blue Mountain Quadrangle

Enchanting is the term to describe this trail. It is not the place for hurrying. If you would relax in the midst of beauty, this is the place to do it.

Access to the trailhead is off Rte. 30 east of Blue Mountain Lake village. At 0.9 m. (1.5 km.) from the intersection of Rte. 28 and 30, 0.6 m. (1.0 km.) past the St. Lawrence and Hudson Rivers Divide sign, turn right onto Durant Road. If coming from the east, Durant Road is 2.3 m. (3.7 km.) past the Lake Durant Public Campsite sign and just past the lake itself. Travel 0.2 m. (0.3 km.) down Durant Road to the trailhead sign on the left side of the road. It is just before you reach a cemetery. Your vehicle may be left here or can be parked a short distance down the trail road. Please do not block the passageway.

From the paved road, follow red DEC trail markers a short distance to where an arrow on a sign points to an abrupt turn to the right. Crossing a small brook, the path follows a level route before ascending a tiny knoll.

The trees are an unusual mix. Large hemlocks overshadow the small balsam firs that are coming in. Before you realize it, you are dropping down a slope to Rock Pond. This extension of Lake Durant is crossed on a 200-ft. (61 m.) wooden bridge. The white lilies, current drawn grasses, and purple spiked pickerel weed give you reason to pause. Gazing out on this quiet water, you understand the meaning of "forever wild."

Continuing on, a short steep section is soon surmounted as you top a little ridge. The trees are now maple and beech. A rather steep, but brief, descent into the next valley brings you to the second joy of this trip.

For the next twenty minutes, you travel 0.5 m. (0.8 km.) up a delicate valley between two high ridges. The trees are of smaller diameter and are further apart here. It is like being in a huge amphitheater. Again you feel a distinct urge to walk slowly, so that you may see everything. It is quite beautiful.

Finally, at the end of the valley, you ascend a moderate slope where the trail becomes essentially level for the remaining 0.9 m. (1.5 km.) to Cascade Pond. You come to a DEC sign 0.5 m. (0.8 km.) from Cascade Pond. Just beyond the sign, bear left. Avoid the unmarked trail to the right.

The trees have now changed to mostly spruce. Cascade Pond is seen at the right a few moments before you reach the lean-to, which sits above the pond. This large beautiful body of water has an active beaver colony.

If a second car is available to the party, a loop ending at the Northville-Placid Trail parking area near the Lake Durant Campsite is possible. By continuing along the pond edge on the red DEC trail for another 0.9 m. (1.5 km.) you will reach the Northville-Placid Trail. Turning left here, blue markers will take you another 2.7 m. (4.4 km.) to the Lake Durant Campsite. There are excellent swimming facilities there. Blue markers will take you past the swimming area and on to the roadside parking location. This would make a total loop of 6.4 m. (10.4 km.).

Rock Pond in summer

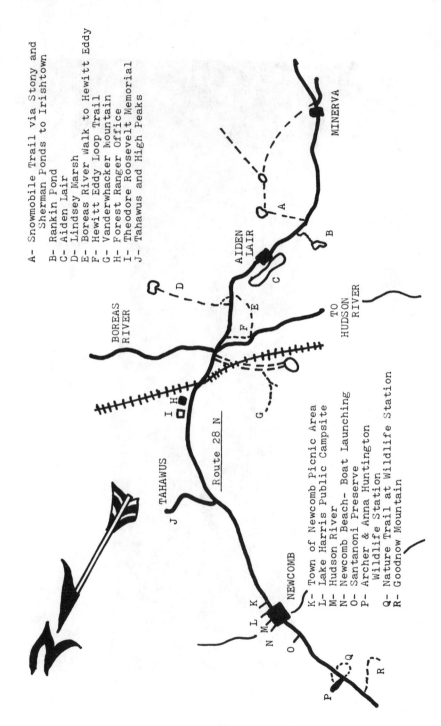

A– Snowmobile Trail via Stony and
    Sherman Ponds to Irishtown
B– Rankin Pond
C– Aiden Lair
D– Lindsey Marsh
E– Boreas River Walk to Hewitt Eddy
F– Hewitt Eddy Loop Trail
G– Vanderwhacker Mountain
H– Forest Ranger Office
I– Theodore Roosevelt Memorial
J– Tahawus and High Peaks

K– Town of Newcomb Picnic Area
L– Lake Harris Public Campsite
M– Hudson River
N– Newcomb Beach– Boat Launching
O– Santanoni Preserve
P– Archer & Anna Huntington
    Wildlife Station
Q– Nature Trail at Wildlife Station
R– Goodnow Mountain

MINERVA

AIDEN
LAIR

BOREAS
RIVER

TO
HUDSON
RIVER

Route 28 N

TAHAWUS

NEWCOMB

MINERVA-NEWCOMB SECTION

The region between Minerva and Newcomb provides an amazing combination of interesting recreational opportunities. To a large extent, it has been ignored as hikers followed the major highway systems into the high peaks. Even those traveling to Tahawus and the complex of trails branching northward to Lake Colden and Mt. Marcy seem not to have been aware of what they were passing by.

Reference to the accompanying drawing will indicate several of the possibilities for outdoor activities. Harris Lake Public Campsite makes a good base for those staying in the area for an extended length of time. Backpackers and cross-country skiers will find Santanoni Preserve very satisfying. There are canoe and boat water access sites both at Newcomb and Harris Lake. Mountains with spectacular views of the high peaks are found here. Charming jaunts into flowering marshes and along gurgling brooks make delightful day trips. All things considered, this is a splendid place to enjoy nature.

The sequence of trips provided in this section begins where the Olmstedville Road intersects Rte. 28N at Minerva. It continues along Rte. 28N northwestward to Newcomb and slightly beyond.

22. RANKIN POND

Round Trip Time—30 min.
Round Trip Distance—0.8 m. (1.3 km.)
Elevation Change—100 ft. (32 km.)
Difficulty—Easy, with some gradual ascent on the return.
Map—Newcomb Quadrangle

A small turnoff, possibly with a signpost, is found at the trailhead on the west side of Rte. 28N, 4.3 m. (6.9 km.) north of Minerva. Parking places are available for a few cars.

Following blue markers, the trail turns abruptly left almost immediately and wends its way through a hardwood forest. It soon begins a gradual descent over a rocky path and quickly reaches the water's edge.

A small shoreline clearing lends a magnificent view of the pond. The distant shore is cloaked with blueberry bushes. Water plants gracefully reach up through the water to the sky above. It's a quiet place and quite beautiful.

23. BOREAS RIVER WALK

Round Trip Time—1 hr. 30 min.
Round Trip Distance—2.2 m. (3.6 km.)
Elevation Change—20 ft. (6 m.)
Difficulty—Easy.
Map—Newcomb Quadrangle

Many years ago there was a state campsite on the Boreas River where it crosses Rte. 28N. Today only a few remaining fireplaces give witness to the past. The river crossing is 8.7 m. (13.9 km.) from Minerva. Recently a new concrete bridge was built across the river. The approach to the old bridge makes a good parking area. It is adjacent to the old campsite.

The trail begins on the west side of the road, opposite the parking area. It follows red DEC markers along the river bank for the whole distance. The stream's varying sounds are intriguing. First silent, then noisily rushing, it continuously whets your curiosity. Numerous little side trails lead to the river's edge and interesting sights. One notices the fragrance of the conifers and the softness of the earth beneath one's feet.

It's hard to imagine that this little stream once carried thousands of logs downstream each spring, as dammed meltwaters were released. Log drivers, mostly French Canadians, nimbly leapt from log to log as they worked to prevent jams.

The trail rambles on with but a single rise above the river. At one point the rushing water draws you to a rocky waterfall. Occasionally a small tributary is crossed.

At the 1.1 m. (1.8 km.) point, the Hewitt Eddy Loop Trail joins the Boreas River Trail at Hewitt Eddy. Do not stray from the river's edge, unless you wish to make the loop hike. The Hewitt Eddy Loop Trail runs 0.75 m. (1.2 km.) further through the woods to Rte. 28N, some 0.6 m. (1.0 km.) south of the Boreas River bridge. If both trails are to be walked, it is suggested that you start at the Hewitt Eddy Loop Trail trailhead.

It was once possible to proceed further down river for a different view of Hewitt Eddy, but that section is no longer maintained.

24. VANDERWHACKER MOUNTAIN

Round Trip Time—5 hrs.
Round Trip Distance—5.8 m. (9.3 km.)
Elevation Change—1650 ft. (495 m.)
Summit Elevation—3385 ft. (1016 m.)
Difficulty—Moderate for experienced hikers,
    possibly challenging for novices.
Map—Newcomb Quadrangle

Named after an early pioneer who lived at the base of the mountain, Vanderwhacker Mountain stands alone. Its summit presents a beautiful vista to the north, where the High Peaks rise.

The approach is a gravel road on the west side of Rte. 28N. This is 8.8 m. (14 km.) from Minerva, just across the Boreas River bridge. A mailbox marks the spot, where a large signpost once stood.

This road immediately climbs a steep loose gravel slope. Once this hazard is surmounted, the remainder of the 2.6 m. (4.2 km.) drive is better. The driver must, however, use normal caution. Traveling through a beautiful coniferous forest, one feels no desire to rush, anyway. Avoid the left hand turn at 1.5 m. (2.4 km.) just before crossing Vanderwhacker Brook on a small bridge. There are several open campsites with picnic tables and fireplaces in this area.

The road bears right, crossing a railroad track. One notices the road narrowing and more care is required from this point onward. At 2.6 m. (4.2 km.), a right turn abruptly brings you to a small parking area, a picnic table, and the trailhead. This is the first turnoff since the railroad tracks and is marked by a very crude sign reading "Vanderwhacker Mountain."

Following red DEC markers, the trail gradually climbs through a hardwood forest. Soon leveling off, it swings right as it skirts a swampy area and crosses two small streams.

More gradual inclines then take you upward for another twenty minutes. Just after crossing a stream at 1.3 m. (2.1 km.), the grade steepens and you can see the fire observer's cabin up the open slope. The snowmobile trail turns left, below the cabin, but the hiking trail passes between the buildings and continues uphill. Situated on a grassy grade, the cabin is a good place to take a rest.

The route leads past the buildings and is much steeper for some distance. Eventually it moderates and finally becomes a path along a narrow ridge. This is a marvelous section of the trail. With the open sky above, and the trees sloping off steeply below on each side, it is exhilarating.

Various small herbs and flowers grow here. Occasional ferns add to the scenery. When present, balmy breezes make the setting complete.

Becoming steeper again, the trail ascends one last stretch before emerging at the small sharp peak. It is closed in by trees on three sides, but open views are clear to the north. The fire tower is again open, and the panorama is most rewarding. Algonquin and Avalanche Pass stand out. Mt. Colden, Redfield, Marcy, Haystack, Allen, Gothics, Sawteeth, Nipple Top, the Boreas Range, Dix, McComb, and countless minor peaks are evident. Plan on staying on top for awhile.

In winter, the approach road would be an excellent cross-country skiing area through to Moose Pond. It also would be a good climb up the mountain on showshoes.

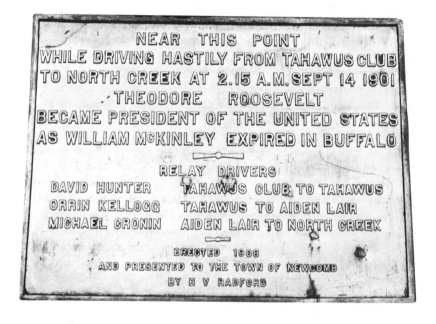

Roosevelt tablet

Roosevelt Memorial Tablet. A stone monument with a metal tablet honoring President Theodore Roosevelt is located on the north side of Rte. 28N, 12.7 m. (20.3 km.) from Minerva.This is 2.2 m. (3.5 km.) from Newcomb.

On September 6, 1901, President McKinley was wounded in an assassination attempt in Buffalo, New York. Assured that McKinley was recovering, Vice-President Roosevelt struck out for the Tahawus Club

68

and Mt. Marcy. On Friday, September 13th, his climbing party, having ascended Mt. Marcy, was enjoying lunch at Lake Tear of the Clouds when a messenger burst out of the woods and informed Roosevelt that McKinley had taken a turn for the worse.

This resulted in a hasty withdrawal to the Tahawus Club and an eventual midnight race by horse-drawn carriage to a train standing by at North Creek, ready to speed him off. The monument marks the approximate spot Roosevelt had reached in his dash through the night when McKinley, at 2:15 a.m. on September 14th, died and Roosevelt became President.

25. ARCHER AND ANNA HUNTINGTON WILDLIFE FOREST STATION NATURE TRAIL
Round Trip Time — 1 hr.
Round Trip Distance — 0.5 m. (0.8 km.)
Elevation Change — 15 ft. (4.6 m.)
Difficulty — Very easy.
Map — Newcomb Quadrangle

This nature trail is located 2.5 m. (4 km.) west of the Santanoni Preserve signpost in Newcomb on Rte. 28N. It is open for use from approximately June 15th until October 15th each year.

The trail has been developed by the students and staff of the SUNY College of Environmental Science and Forestry of Syracuse University. The station is a research unit of the college. A parking area and small building where trail guides are kept are found at the beginning of the trail.

Though only about 0.5 m. (0.8 km.) long, the trail is well-designed. Numbered markers along the route correlate with the guide book to help identify plant life. Beaver dams, spruce flats, and glacial boulders may be seen. Over 170 species of birds have been sighted in this area, and the most commonly observed ones are listed. Leaf drawings simplify the identification of trees.

This is an especially nice place for young children to visit. The distance is short enough to retain their attention and the experience can be most educational. It is an excellent opportunity for parents to teach good forest behavior. Remember the saying, "Take only pictures and leave only footprints."

26. GOODNOW MOUNTAIN

Round Trip Time — 2 hrs. 15 min.
Round Trip Distance — 3.0 m. (4.8 km.)
Elevation Change — 1060 ft. (324 m.)
Summit Elevation — 2685 ft. (806 m.)
Difficulty — Easy for experienced hikers,
   moderate to easy for novices.
Map — Newcomb Quadrangle

Perhaps no other mountain in the Adirondacks offers such a rich reward for so little effort. This marvelous little mountain is truly a gem. A small sign on the south side of Rte. 28N, 4 m. (6.4 km.) west of the Santanoni Preserve sign in Newcomb marks the trailhead. The trail is closed each year **from October 15th** until the end of big game hunting season. No motorized equipment is allowed. Hikers are to keep on the trail, since this is private property.

The trail follows red markers over land of the Archer and Anna Huntington Wildlife Forest Station. The gravel road you initially follow bears to the right after only about 150 ft. (45 m.), but the summit trail goes straight ahead up a moderate slope. Becoming a moderately steep grade, the climbing is steady for about 15 minutes on a hard-packed track. The welcome leveling-off that follows gives you a breather.

Maple, birch, and other hardwoods make up the larger growth. These trees generally appear in an orderly plant succession after the original wood has been lumbered. The specific tree species present and their diameter tell something of how long ago the cutting took place. Notice the occasional red spruce sprouting up here and there. It is a sign that the native trees are gradually reclaiming their land.

The trail swings around a very large boulder on the left. Quite a bit of corduroy (wooden cross ties) is seen. Becoming steeper, again, the trail traverses some bare rock. Turning abruptly to the right and widening to a tote road, the trail passes a metal storage shed on the right. An open view can be obtained from a rock outcrop behind this building.

The woods open up as the tote road winds its curving course upward. Easily traveled, this section is rather attractive. Massive rocks form cliffs on the right, with beds of fern at their feet. A short path leads to the right, where an old covered well stands. The road now curves back to the left. An arrow on a Goodnow Mountain sign directs you to a narrowing path where a second building is passed.

Your route is now along the side of a ridge and is a pleasant journey. Views begin to open up. In a few moments, you drop down into a small col. Avoid a side trail to the left which follows the col downward. Far below in the distance is Rich Lake. Its deep blue is in sharp contrast to the emerald green of the forest trees.

A tower sign points straight ahead and another five minutes along this trail brings you to the fire tower and the cabin of the observer. The mountain is fairly open on its rocky top. Absolutely spectacular views are available to the west, north and east. Climbing the fire tower extends your sighting radius to a full 360 degrees.

Quite literally, all of the high peaks are visible past the beautiful waters of Rich Lake. To the east, Vanderwhacker's fire tower can be spotted. Far to the west, Long Lake flows northward. As Robert Wickam once said while speaking of another area, "After gazing awhile, the inclination comes to murmur amen."

It would seem that a winter trip up Goodnow Mountain would be tremendously interesting. The trail is wide and easily followed. It is a short trip, but Santanoni Preserve is near by, if additional exercise is desired.

High Peaks from Goodnow Mountain

71

27. BOREAS MOUNTAIN

Round Trip Time—4 hrs. 30 min.
Round Trip Distance—6.7 m. (10.9 km.)
Elevation Change—1925 ft. (589 m.)
Summit Elevation—3776 ft. (1155 m.)
Difficulty—Easy to moderately challenging in places.
Maps—Mt. Marcy and Schroon Lake Quadrangles

The first part of the hike winds through a beautiful forest. The second part trudges up a hardscrabble road that is gradually growing over with grass. The last portion of the hike is up a moderate to steep grade on the mountain trail. The view is excellent in two directions through the tree openings. There is a closed fire tower. It is rapidly deteriorating and is not safe to climb.

The approach is made off Blue Ridge Road, which runs west from Exit 29 on the Adirondack Northway (Rte. 87). It connects up with Rte. 28N a short distance along the Tahawus Road. Four miles (6.5 km.) west of Exit 29, turn north onto Elk Lake Road. A large sign for Elk Lake Lodge marks the turn. This good gravel road proceeds 3.3 m. (5.3 km.) to the Boreas Mountain trailhead at Clear Pond. A small sign marks the location where there is parking space for a few cars.

This trail goes over private land. Take care to preserve its quality. Following red trail markers, the trail enters the woods and gradually descends through a fragrant conifer and hardwood forest. It comes into a grassy old tote road at 0.3 m. (0.5 km.) and turns left. The Elk Lake outlet (The Branch) is crossed on a rustic old bridge. From its center, the fire tower on the mountain can be seen.

This delightful path continues to where it crosses a stream on logs at 0.8 m. (1.3 km.). A small lane from the right soon merges with the trail, a clearing is reached, and then a large grassy road crosses from the right. A few old signs may be found on trees here. The route to the right leads back to Elk Lake Lodge.

Continue straight ahead up the grassy grade. Watch for an abrupt turn to the left, as the path nears a stream on the right. A sharp pitch upward brings you to the hardscrabble road. *Note this place, so you won't walk past it on the return trip.* Turning right, take this road northward for about a mile (1.6 km.). The grade is steadily upward. Avoid a road left, a road right, and another road to the left. Trail markers are well placed, so there shouldn't be any difficulty. Along the way one has another good view of the fire tower. Crossing a few streams may create minor problems in wet weather.

The fire observer's cabin is reached at 2.5 m. (4.1 km.). A cool stream flows behind the cabin and a small grove of apple trees is in the clearing to the front. It is a good place for a lunch break.

The trail continues to the left of the cabin and crosses the brook. It begins to climb in earnest for the rest of the way. Because it is an old trail, soil has eroded down to bare rock in places. In wet weather, much water will be found, but this will not present any real obstacle. A spring is passed on the left at 2.9 m. (4.7 km.)

A rather steep section, just beyond the spring, soon becomes easier. The summit is reached at 3.4 m. (5.5 km.). Two breathtaking views are seen through openings looking out from the otherwise wooded peak. You feel as if you're sitting on top of the world, since the peak is truly a small area. The first view is northeast over Elk Lake. McComb, Hough, and Dix are in line. Nipple Top is at the end of Elk Lake, with Colvin and Blake to its left. The second view, more to the left, is toward Mt. Marcy and the mountains that surround it.

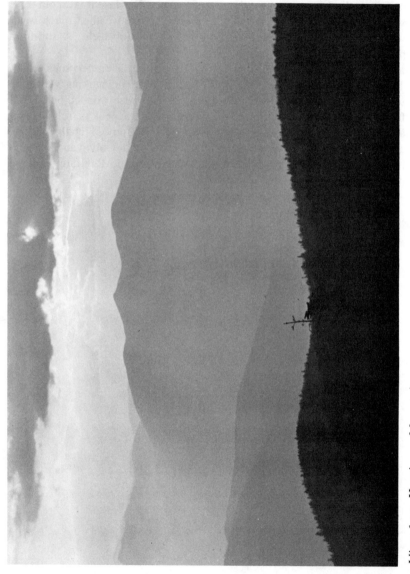

View from Hurricane Mountain

KEENE—KEENE VALLEY SECTION

The Keene-Keene Valley Section epitomizes the Adirondacks for mountain climbers. It is in this region that many of the "High Peaks," those over 4000 ft. (1223 m.), are found. It is here that Orson Schofield "Old Mountain" Phelps had the feeling of "heaven up-h'istedness" as he gazed from "O'Mercy" (Mt. Marcy).

This results in a curious imbalance, however. While the masses are climbing the giants, the most casual glance at a map will indicate dozens of other peaks that are nearly neglected. If these "little giants" were in other parts of the Adirondacks, they would be scaled far more frequently. It is from these oft-forgotten mountains that many of the truly panoramic views of the Adirondack Range are found. The hikes described here are representative of the variety of outing opportunities in this region.

Access to this section is by Rtes. 73 and 9N.

28. THE BROTHERS TRAIL AND LOOP OPTION
Round Trip Time—5 hrs.
Round Trip Distance—5.0 m. (8.1 m.)
Elevation Change—2198 ft. (672 m.)
Summit Elevation—3721 ft. (1138 m.)
Difficulty—Moderately difficult, but steep in one place.
Map—Mt. Marcy Quadrangle

The following trail description is in two parts. The hiker who wants absolutely beautiful scenery in the context of an afternoon jaunt over bare rock is advised to take the hike up to the summit of The Third Brother. On the other hand, the well-conditioned hiker who wants a full day's trip couldn't choose a nicer way to spend the day than to tramp the loop option.

Access to the trailhead is off Rte. 73. Turn at the large DEC "Trails to the High Peaks" sign in the village of Keene Valley. Drive 1.6 m. (2.6 km.) to the parking area, called The Garden. The Garden is one of three primary points of entry into the High Peaks.

It may be well to point out that at The Garden some of the obvious contrasts between High Peaks hiking and hiking in other areas of the Adirondacks will be felt. You'll immediately realize that many people are using the area. Finding a parking place may be difficult. A park ranger may be on duty here to help and advise hikers.

Before starting out, be sure that you have plenty of drinking water, since there will be little along the way.

The trail begins at the right rear corner of the parking area, following red ADK markers up a moderately steep slope. Be careful not to take the yellow Phelps trail, which starts at the left rear of the parking area.

The grade soon levels to a moderate grade and a pleasant walk takes you through the white birches above Juliet Brook. After twenty minutes, the trail turns left and drops down to the stream. Soon after crossing Juliet Brook, the hardest climbing of the trip begins. Becoming a steep grade, the trail swings to the left between two boulders. Emerging at rock outlooks, you have excellent views of Hurricane Mountain to the northeast and Giant to the east. Mt. Marcy is in the southeast.

From 1.2 m. (1.9 km.) onward, there is mostly open rock climbing to the flat summit of First Brother. Here, Johns Brook Valley spreads before you. Across the valley the Great Range of Lower and Upper Wolf Jaw, Armstrong, and Gothics are seen.

The trail descends slightly and then continues gradually upward to the summit of Second Brother. A good outlook is found 20 yds. (18 m.) off the trail to the right.

The path enters trees and drops through a birch and fern woods. From here it again heads upward toward the summit of the Third Brother. The appearance of balsam fir tells you that higher elevations are being reached. From the Third Brother, which is more closed in than were the other summits, the profile of the bare slide of Big Slide Mountain stands out before you. There is no other peak quite like Big Slide in all of these mountains. *The afternoon hiker is advised to go no further.* The return route provides different perspectives of interesting scenery.

The well conditioned hiker who wishes a longer trip may well continue. The whole loop from The Garden takes approximately seven hours to complete. From this point onward, the trail is harder to navigate and is in poorer condition.

The continuing path drops into a balsam fir and spruce forest. At 2.7 m. (4.4 km.) a natural rock shelter is seen on the left. The col is reached fifteen minutes later. A gradual climb to the junction with Slide Brook Trail now begins.

The junction is reached at 3.6 m (5.8 km.). From here, the hiker may turn right for another optional side trip. It is an extremely steep 0.3 m. (0.5 km.) to the summit of Big Slide Mountain. If you have the energy, it is worth the extra time to make the trip.

Turning left down the Slide Brook Trail, descend the slopes through berry bushes to the floor of Johns Brook Valley. Following Slide Brook, views of the Great Range are frequently seen through the trees across the valley. A spring is passed, soon after beginning this stretch, but it cannot always be counted on to have water. Slide Brook appears halfway down the slope and is crossed and recrossed many times.

When the Phelps Trail is reached, a left turn takes you back toward your starting place at The Garden. However, the hiker may wish to turn right and take the short ten-minute walk to Johns Brook Lodge (JBL). JBL, a wilderness lodge owned and operated by the Adirondack Mountain Club, is unique to the Adirondacks and well worth seeing.

Yellow markers take you along Johns Brook as you return toward The Garden. Soon after crossing Slide Brook for the last time, you will see Howard lean-to on the right. Another few minutes down the trail and a trail junction is reached at the ranger's cabin. Take the branch to the left and continue following yellow markers.

Rolling terrain with occasionally moderate grades will be traversed for the last 3.0 m. (4.9 km.) of this outing. This attractive, though heavily traveled, section passes through hardwood forests.

1.4 m. (2.3 km.) from The Garden, three large boulders are reached. One is often used for emergency shelter, as the blackened smoke on the overhang indicates. Deer Brook lean-to is soon reached after a short, steep little climb from the brook. Another fifteen minutes of walking brings you to Bear Brook lean-to. From here, a persistent decline in elevation eases the way for the last 0.9 m. (1.5 km.) to the Garden.

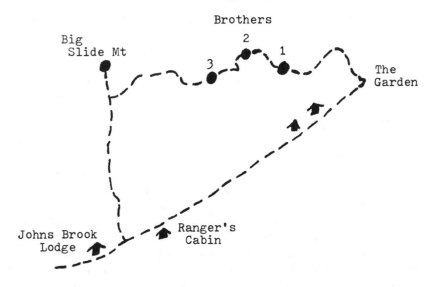

THE BROTHERS LOOP TRAIL

29. HOPKINS MOUNTAIN via MOSSY CASCADE BROOK

Round Trip Time—4 hrs. 30 min.
Round Trip Distance—6.3 m. (10.3 km.)
Elevation Change—2120 ft. (648 m.)
Summit Elevation—3183 ft. (973 m.)
Difficulty—Moderate, perhaps challenging for the novice.
Map—Mount Marcy and Elizabethtown Quadrangles

The walk to the waterfalls on Mossy Cascade Brook is charming. The climb along the brook through hemlocks, frequent lookouts, and seasonal blueberries add to the pleasure. It is topped off with an open summit, from which 22 major peaks are visible up through Ausable Lakes and Johns Brook valleys.

The trailhead is off Rte. 73, 0.4 m. (0.6 km.) towards Keene Valley from the Ausable Club entrance sign at St. Huberts. Park at the next St. Huberts side road, 0.1 m. (0.2 km.) from the trailhead. A green and white ATIS signpost and trail markers on the north side of Rte. 73, where the bank drops from the road, mark the trail.

The trail crosses Crystal Brook and then follows above the East Branch of the Ausable through woods until it nears a home at the left at 0.4 m. (0.6 km.). Swinging right, onto a tote road, it immediately turns left to another old road. Finally, the trail bears right at a junction and curves southeast over flat terrain.

The trail leaves the road at 0.5 m. (0.8 km.) and follows the left bank of Mossy Cascade Brook. (Soon a side path is seen that leads 200 yds. to the left before reaching the base of Mossy Cascade Brook Falls.) The summit trail bears right, passes to the left of a private camp, and then heads up several steep pitches.

The first open lookout is reached at 1.5 m. (2.4 km.). The route then descends into a col before climbing to another broad ledge where more viewing is possible.

The trail moderates before reaching the Ranney Trail junction at 2.3 m. (3.7 km.). (The Ranney Trail heads left 1.8 m., 2.9 km., to Keene Valley.) The route enters a ravine between Hopkins and Green mountains. It reaches another junction at 3.0 m. (4.9 km.). Turn left. (The trail right leads 3.0 m., 4.9 km., to the summit of Giant Mountain.)

The trail climbs very steeply from this junction for a short distance. It then moderates and runs over open rock to the summit. The view up Ausable Lakes Valley and Johns Brook Valley is magnificent. Enjoy lunch and don't eat all the blueberries.

From the summit, a trail leads northwest 0.7 m. (1.1 km.) to the lookout near the summit of Spread Eagle Mountain and then another 1.7 m. (2.8 km.) to the Beede Road trailhead in Keene Valley.

30. HURRICANE MOUNTAIN
Round Trip Time—4 hrs. 30 min.
Round Trip Distance—5.3 m. (8.6 km.)
Elevation Change—2000 ft. (611 m.)
Summit Elevation—3694 ft. (1130 m.)
Difficulty—A moderate rate of climb for a fairly
   long ascent distance.
Map—Elizabethtown Quadrangle

The Indian name for Hurricane Mountain is *No-do-ne-yo*, Hill of Wind. Its vast bulk is often buffeted by strong air currents. Alfred Billings Street, the famous lawyer and librarian of 19th century Adirondackana, commented on this wind in his book, *The Indian Pass*. "It put me in mind of the Scripture question, 'What went ye out in the wilderness to see? A reed shaken with the wind?' No, but a crest shaken (nearly) with a whirlwind. Most appropriately named is that peak. The wind fairly poured a torrent over it. I have an indistinct recollection of dim shapes and fluttering garments huddling together for mutual protection from the wolfish blasts, while I clutched the rim of my hat with the clutch of desperation. But the view was superb." Carry a jacket or sweater with you for comfort at the summit. Pick a good day and enjoy that superb view. It's one of the best in the mountains.

The trailhead is on the north side of Rte. 9N, 3.6 m. (5.8 km.) east from Rte. 73 and 1.6 m. (2.6 km.) past Hurricane Road. This is 6.8 m. (11.0 km.) west from Elizabethtown. It is marked by a small DEC signpost and there is a parking area on the opposite side of the road.

The trail follows red DEC trail markers. It immediately climbs steeply up from the road for about fifteen minutes. Then leveling off, the way becomes a footpath. Passing through a pretty coniferous forest, two streams are crossed on bridges before a minor wet area is reached. Beyond this two more bridges are crossed. Be sure you have enough water before leaving this last stream, since you may not find any more on the trail.

Having traveled easily a little over a mile (1.8 km.), climbing now becomes more challenging. Heading up a ridge, long moderate grades with periodic respites take you upward. Take care to follow markers straight up the mountain when you reach the small blowdown section. Do not extend the false trail to the left, as some earlier hikers have done. Another wet section is crossed on corduroy as you approach the 2.0 m. (3.2 km.) point.

Once past this section, climbing picks up again. The change from coniferous to birch trees at this elevation is a reminder of past forest fires. Just before joining the ADK North Trail from the Mountain House, the trail again steepens sharply and is quite rocky.

Turning right at this junction, the trail levels and the last 265 yds. (243 m.) to the summit passes through wind stunted spruces to the bare rock. Paint blazes now take you generally to the left and guide you to the base of the fire tower. A full circle panorama makes it unnecessary to climb the tower.

To the north you can see the Jay Range. The Green Mountains of Vermont spread out beyond Lake Champlain in the northeast. Directly southward is Knob Lock, with the ridge of Green Mountain beyond it. Giant and Rocky Peak Ridge are still further off. Dix, Nipple Top, the Great Range, and finally Mt. Marcy are seen as your gaze swings southwestward. Mt. Colden and the MacIntyre Range are next seen. These are followed by Cascade and Porter. Pitchoff is due west, with distant Ampersand just to its left. Whiteface Mountain is northwest. Lesser peaks, too numerous to list, are found in all directions.

31. BALANCED ROCKS ON PITCHOFF MOUNTAIN
Round Trip Time — 2 hrs. 30 mins.
Round Trip Distance — 3.1 m. (5.0 km.)
Elevation Change — 882 ft. (270 m.)
Summit Elevation — 3022 ft. (924 m.)
**Difficulty — Half is easy, half is on a very
    steep eroded trail.**
Map — Mt. Marcy Quadrangle

The Balanced Rocks on Pitchoff Mountain provide both a climb and viewing location that are quite unusual. The hiker should be prepared for some steep climbing and an eroded trail. The small ridge that holds the

Balanced rocks, Pitchoff Mountain

Balanced Rocks has an appearance more of the Swiss Alps than of the Adirondacks. Expect an interesting outing.

Access to the trailhead is off Rte. 73 at the north end of Upper Cascade Lake. This is 4.5 m. (7.3 km.) east of Heart Lake Road. Park in the area provided at the Cascade Mountain trailhead and climb the Pitchoff Mountain trail directly across the road.

Red DEC trail markers take you up a moderately steep grade for about five minutes. The route then levels for the next 0.5 m. (0.8 km.). You first find an attractive open maple stand and then a spruce-birch wood.

About twenty minutes after starting your climb, you ascend a steep pitch to a small lookout at the right. Cascade Mountain stands out. Another longer pitch brings you to a better lookout, where both Cascade Lakes are clearly seen in their glory below. The sharp cut in Cascade

81

Mountain between the two lakes was the original trail up that peak. It leads to the cascade of water from which the mountain gets its name.

Moving along the ridge side, you soon drop down to a flattened depression, which is quickly crossed. Steep climbing then begins. After ascending one such section, the trail swings left on the level for a short distance. A second steep eroded section follows, until you reach the bare rock face of a near vertical slope at 1.1 m. (1.8 km.).

The old trail to the right is considered dangerous. The safer route follows red markers to the left. Here, you spend the next fifteen minutes sidling around the bald wall of the mountain. You soon descend slightly, and then begin a moderate, but steady, climb to the upper end of the rock massif. It is reached at 1.4 m. (2.3 km.).

Turn right for Balanced Rocks. On a welcome level stretch the whole character of your surroundings makes a dramatic metamorphosis. Low conifers thin out as you move toward the end of the ridge. A barren, windswept aura of desolation develops. Void of vegetation, the two great Balanced Rocks perch at the extreme point of the ridge, seemingly ready to fall into the great abyss below. Giant eroded joint patterns in the rock floor give the whole scene an appearance of being ready to collapse at any moment, but they have been this way for millenniums. Beyond the Balanced Rocks, the ridge's vast rounded edge juts toward Lake Placid in the distance.

To the left, Cascade Mountain stands, overshadowing all else. Algonquin is seen behind her, along with Big Slide, Colden, and Marcy. Hurricane is in the east. Behind you the first summit of Pitchoff sticks up.

This is a good place to have lunch. You may want to walk a short way south of the Balanced Rocks to where a splendid view of the Cascade Lakes can be seen from a ledge.

The trip can be extended on a pretty trail by continuing from the junction on up to the first peak of Pitchoff Mountain. The trail narrows considerably and is quite easy. The round trip to the summit and back to the junction will add another forty-five minutes and 1.1 m. (1.8 km.) to your outing. The summit elevation is 3600 ft. (1101 m.).

Stagecoach Rock. There is a little-known monument between Lake Placid and Keene. It commemorates the passing of the day of the stagecoach in the Adirondacks. Some 4.6 m. (7.5 km.) east of Heart Lake Road, the boulder is found at a pulloff on the north side of Rte. 73. This is just downhill from the trailhead to Cascade Mountain, across the road from Upper Cascade Lake. Here, carved into the large rock, are a stagecoach, team, and driver.

Stagecoach Rock

From 1855 to 1890, the stagecoach was the primary means of public conveyance in the mountains. The main stations were Elizabethtown, Keesville, Ausable Forks, and North Creek. From these locations, routes spread out through the North Country to interior towns and resort hotels.

For fifteen years, Fred Cook drove six horses over the treacherous Spruce Hill Road from Elizabethtown. "Fitch" O'Brien hauled passengers up through the much feared Wilmington Notch. Ike Roblee headed up to Blue Mountain and Long Lake from North Creek. Dozens of other skilled drivers safely carried their charges through the woods until the "iron horse" and "horseless carriage" put them to pasture. An era had ended.

One day in the 1930's Mr. Donald Rogers, a district engineer working on highways, was at work when a large boulder fell to the roadside off Pitchoff Mountain. Thinking it too nice to simply push aside, he had the forethought to seek a use for it. Eventually Louis Brown of Carnes Granite Co., Inc. drew up a sketch and Wilfred Carnes sandblasted the outline of the stagecoach and team on the boulder. It is a fitting tribute of the highway department to a mode of transportation found in another era. The people of the Adirondacks take pride in their heritage.

32. NOONMARK MOUNTAIN FROM ROUND POND
Round Trip Time — 5 hrs.
Round Trip Distance — 6.7 m. (10.9 km.)
Elevation Change — 1991 ft. (609 m.)
Summit Elevation — 3556 ft. (1087 m.)
Difficulty — A steady climb of fair effort.
Maps — Elizabethtown and Mt. Marcy Quadrangles

Noonmark gets its name because the Sun stands directly over it at noon, as viewed from Keene Valley. This middle-sized peak presents a panorama of great beauty. From its bare rock pinnacle most of the major peaks can be seen.

Access to the trailhead is the Round Pond Trail off Rte. 73. This is 1.1 m. (1.8 km.) southeast of Chapel Pond and 3.0 m. (4.9 km.) northwest of the intersection of Rtes. 9 and 73. It is on the southwest side of the road. A large parking area is just north of the trailhead.

The 0.6 m. (1.0 km.) hike into Round Pond is a moderate but steady climb over a well-used route. During the ten minute walk, you follow red DEC trail markers to the top of a grade and then drop down toward the pond. Before reaching the camping area at the water's edge, the trail turns right. It begins a level swing around the north shore of the water. This pretty section has an unusual amount of both white birch and cedars.

Pulling away from the pond, a steady ascent begins. For the next half hour the trail changes from a moderate to a moderately steep slope, following a stream up a col on the south edge of Round Mountain. At 1.6 m. (2.6 km.), the trail levels, then descends slightly and finally levels again. A junction is reached at 2.3 m. (3.8 km.).

The blue-marked Dix Trail from St. Huberts crosses your route here. A stream provides the last sure water. Orange ATIS (Adirondack Trail Improvement Society) trail markers take you straight ahead, up the Felix Adler Trail toward the summit of Noonmark. Moderately steep to steep grades are found on this eroded section of trail. Some interesting rock cuts are passed through.

About a half hour later, the first lookout is reached as bare rock and spruces appear. Dix Mountain and Nippletop are seen to the south. As elevation is gained, several more lookouts are passed. Soon Round Top, Giant, and Rocky Peak Mountains are seen to the right, to the northeast. The trees decrease in both number and size. Then, one last rise takes you to the bald summit. The whole high peak region is before you.

The emerald carpet of conifers spreads out toward the Great Range. Gothics is spectacular. Mt. Marcy is to the left of Gothics. Beyond the Great Range, Johns Brook Valley and The Brothers are seen. The Dix Range is to the south. Hunter's Pass sharply cuts between Dix Mountain and Nippletop. Spend a long time on this summit.

33. THE CROWS MOUNTAINS
Round Trip Time — 3 hrs.
Round Trip Distance — 2.7 m. (4.4 km.)
Elevation Change — 1220 ft. (373 m.)
Summit Elevation — 2800 ft. (856 m.)
Difficulty — Steep but short.
Maps — Elizabethtown and Ausable Forks
    Quadrangles or Lake Placid and Lewis
    Quadrangles (1:25,000 metric)

The joy of these two small peaks is the immense amount of open-rock climbing that is found here. Excellent views are available for the time expended. Take a good book and spend a long afternoon on top of the world.

Access to the trailhead is off East Hill Road from the village of Keene. The ADK trailhead is on the north side of the road, 2.1 m. (3.4 km.) from Keene. Note the mileage carefully, since the trailhead sign is on a tree just a few feet off the road. Parking is found a little further down the road from the trailhead. The Mountain House is also 0.23 m. (0.3 km.) beyond the trail.

The trail wends its way through an open hardwood stand to a pine woods. Red ADK markers then take you on a fifteen minute steady climb to the beginning of the rocks. You pass a large boulder, a huge U-shaped rock, and an immense oak tree.

Turning right, at a vertical rock face, you start angling up the side of Little Crow Mountain. The Trail is now almost entirely over rock. Outlooks soon appear as you very rapidly gain elevation. Cairns and paint blazes mark much of the way. Passing below the west summit of Little Crow, you next reach the flat easy summit.

An unmarked cairn junction is found here. It is easy to miss. Cairns lead left to a very large rock pile, at 0.9 m. (1.5 km.), indicating the true summit. Summit elevation is 2540 ft. (778 m.) and the ascent has been 960 ft. (294 m.). The cairns then lead back to the trail over to Big Crow Mountain. Had you followed the cairns to the right of the junction instead of going to the Little Crow Summit, they would have led you to this location.

Big Crow Mountain stands before you. You must carefully follow the cairns and markers as you drop down to the wooded col between the two peaks.

Steep climbing then takes you up the meandering route to the bare summit of Big Crow Mountain. It is a beautiful spot. Directly back over Little Crow, huge Cascade Mountain looms in the distance. To the left, down the valley, Giant is seen. Further left, in the southeast, Hurricane Mountain is easily located because of its fire tower. Much closer, to the north, is the Nun-da-ga-o Ridge (Soda Range).

Many options are possible for the return trip. The reverse of the ascent is suggested if only one vehicle is available to the party. If you have a second vehicle, a most enjoyable descent can be made to the south, ending at Big Crow Clearing. The second vehicle could be left there by turning left onto O'Toole Road just past the Mountain House. The clearing is the state's trailhead for this mountain and is 1.2 m. (1.9 km.) up O'Toole Road. Of course, you can make this loop even if you don't have a second vehicle. However, it means walking on a dirt road for part of the way.

THE LAKE PLACID AND
SARANAC LAKE SECTION

The Lake Placid and Saranac Lake Section is distinct because it is the transition zone of the two Adirondack land divisions. To the south and east of Lake Placid lie the high peaks of the Mountain Belt. Beyond the Saranacs to the west is the Lake Region.

It was this beautiful setting that attracted such greats as Ralph Waldo Emerson, Louis Agassiz, and William James Stillman in the mid-1800's. What fascinating conversations must have echoed across the waters at their "philosophers' camp" on Follensby Pond and later at Ampersand Pond. It took the Civil War to prevent this group from continuing its summer gathering.

The country is just as inviting today as it was in yesteryear. Many hikers combine canoeing with their tramping here.

34. AMPERSAND MOUNTAIN
Round Trip Time — 4 hrs. 30 min.
Round Trip Distance — 5.4 m. (8.7 km.)
Elevation Change — 1775 ft. (543 m.)
Summit Elevation — 3352 ft. (1025 m.)
Difficulty — First half is easy, second half
**   very steep and rugged.**
Map — Santanoni Quadrangle

Standing on Ampersand Mountain, a hiker can gaze into the bold face of the Seward Range and then to the more distant high peaks. Turning around, he can look below to the Saranacs and the lake country. Such a contrast in beauty is not available to this degree anywhere else in the Adirondacks. This bald summit has long been a favorite, though your reward must be earned.

The trailhead is located on Rte. 3, 12 m. (19.4 km.) east of Tupper Lake and 8 m. (13 km.) south of Saranac Lake Village. A large parking area is on the north side of the road, with the trailhead signpost on the south side. Dropping over the back edge of the parking area is a 0.5 m. (0.8 km.) trail leading to a lean-to on Middle Saranac Lake. This is an

Wanika Falls

attractive camping location. A crescent shaped beach of the "amber-sand," from which this region is thought to have gained its name, makes an after climb swim hard to resist.

The trail begins at a barred gate. Past it, a broad path takes you along a level route through a woods having an almost park-like quality. For twenty minutes, the beauty of well spaced hemlocks keeps your interest. A few gurgling brooks are crossed before a long section of corduroy indicates that changing terrain is ahead.

With the crossing of a shorter, second section of corduroy moderate climbing begins. At 1.6 m. (2.2 km.), the summit can be seen above the trees, just before you arrive at the remains of the fire observer's cabin, in a small clearing. Here, Dutton Brook provides the last sure water. Avoid the old trail that goes straight ahead across the brook at this point.

The new trail swings to the right side of the clearing and follows the creek for a way. A short section of blowdown is easily bypassed.

The last mile (1.6 km.) to the summit is very rugged. Over 1300 vertical feet (398 m.) must be scaled on a poor trail. Tree roots, steep dirt sections, and rocky stream bed conditions demand your constant attention.

Finally, at 2.4 m. (3.9 km.), a col provides a level respite. An extremely large rock overhang is passed under. The trail circles the summit and then a short section of moderately steep grade brings you to the bare rock. Yellow painted markers lead you up the massive rock to the peak.

To your left, in the west, the Saranacs spread out before you. Middle Saranac is smallest and has several islands. Upper Saranac is behind it. Lower Saranac is to its right toward the north. Northeast is Oseetah Lake, with Scarface Mountain at its right. Haystack and McKenzie are beyond Scarface. Whiteface Mountain is still further off to the northeast. Below you to the southeast is Ampersand Pond. Beyond the pond stands Seward Mountain and, to its left, is Mt. Seymour. Imagine, if you will, a little firecracker of a man snowshoeing up Ouluska Pass between those two mountains. He is headed for Coreys on his annual visit to civilization at Christmas time. Such a man actually existed. His name was Noah John Rondeau and he did this every year for over a quarter of a century.

Closer in, to the left of Ampersand Pond, is Van Dorrien Mountain. Just over its shoulder Algonquin is seen, thrusting 5114 ft. (1564 m.) skyward in the distance. To the south is Kempshall Mountain on Long Lake.

Yellow paint markers take you on a short distance to a slightly lower part of the summit. It is here that the foundation supports of the old fire tower can still be found. Nearby, a bronze plate is attached to the rock. It commemorates Walter Channing Rice, "the hermit of Ampersand," who manned the tower for many, many years.

This mountain is often climbed on snowshoes in the winter, though some considerable skill is needed for the last mile.

35. BAKER MOUNTAIN

Round Trip Time—2 hrs.
Round Trip Distance—1.8 m. (2.9 km.)
Elevation Change—884 ft. (270 m.)
Summit Elevation—2452 ft. (750 m.)
Difficulty—Short, but steep; tough little climb.
Map—Saranac Lake Quadrangle (1:125,000) or
     Saranac Lake Quadrangle (1:25,000 metric)

This mountain was almost not included in this book because of its relatively short length. However, after climbing it, it was decided that what it lacked in distance, it made up in steepness. The view is excellent.

Access to the trailhead is off Rte. 86 in Saranac Lake village. Turn right at the traffic island as you enter the village from Lake Placid. Cross the railroad tracks and turn left onto Pine Street, a dirt road. Follow Pine Street, crossing the tracks again, until you reach East Pine Street. Turn right, again crossing the tracks on an overpass. Follow the paved East Pine Street to the north end of Moody Pond. The trailhead is 0.2 m. (0.3 km.) past a small bathing area, set off by a rustic fence. Parking is on the right side of the road.

The beginning of the trail is not marked. Care should be taken to follow directions. The general rule is that when there is a choice of paths to follow, take the one that shows more use.

The trail starts up an old tote road but leaves it almost immediately. A path leads to the right, up a very short grade to a second tote road. Turning left, walk about 100 ft. (32 m.) to where the trail branches to the right, at a junction. This road goes straight along a slight grade over a hardscrabble road. It soon arrives at another fork. Avoid following the road to the right, which has a posted sign on a tree. Take the left fork onto a dirt trail. It skirts the right side of an abandoned quarry. After a few yards, the trail branches to the right on a broad path. Avoid following the rim of the quarry.

Once through this short section, which only covers about 0.1 m. (0.2 km.), the way to the summit is clear. It is up. Moderately steep to steep grades take you along your way for a few minutes. Then a welcome level stretch lets you catch your breath. You are ready for the very steep part, which appears at 0.6 m. (1.0 km.)

The trail is wide and not at all dangerous, but take your time. It is a rather long section of steady climbing. Becoming more rocky, the first red ADK trail markers are now seen. Follow them carefully.

A series of lookouts give excellent views of the high peaks to the southeast. Ampersand Mountain is seen to the south, just beyond large Otseetah Lake. The summit provides a good view eastward. Haystack Mountain is seen across McKenzie Pond. The long hulk of McKenzie Mountain is close behind Haystack Mountain. A short path leads north of the summit to a cliff of considerable height. From it you can see St. Regis Mountain, the large bulk of Debar Mountain, and a few other of the outlying peaks to the north. In all, this amazing little peak looks out to 28 major mountains.

36. HAYSTACK MOUNTAIN
Round Trip Time—5 hrs.
Round Trip Distance—6.6 m. (10.7 km.)
Elevation Change—1240 ft. (379 m.)
Summit Elevation—2878 ft. (880 m.)
Difficulty—A very moderate hike, with short steep sections near end.
Map—Saranac Lake Quadrangle (1:125,000) or Saranac Lake Quadrangle (1:25,000 metric)

It seems there are as many Haystack Mountains in the Adirondacks as there are Mud Lakes. This one is in Ray Brook, near Saranac Lake. The peak is overshadowed by huge McKenzie Mountain, but offers a better view for a lot less effort. In fact, the whole trip is about as nice a day hike as anyone could ask for. The view from the top is excellent.

The old trailhead behind DEC Region 5 Headquarters in Ray Brook was moved in 1984. Today, the trailhead is at a road pulloff on Rte. 86, 1.6 m. (2.6 km.) east of the DEC Headquarters building and 1.4 m. (2.3 km.) west of the junction with Old Military Road. The trailhead has a DEC sign and blue DEC trail markers.

The trail quickly crosses a small knoll and a wet area. Swinging left, gradual climbing takes you over two crests before you drop to a small stream at 0.5 m. (0.8 km.).

Turning left across the creek, the route gradually gains elevation along the base of some low ledges to a point where another slight descent begins at 1.1 m. (1.8 km.). A small clearing at 1.5 m. (2.4 km.) offers viewing to the southwest. Then, at 1.8 m. (2.9 km.), the trail merges with the original trail, which comes in from the left.

The old woods road takes you up a grade beside Little Ray Brook to a junction at 2.4 m. (3.9 km.). The Haystack Mountain trail bears left, continuing on the level. Avoid the McKenzie Mountain trail, which climbs to the right.

View from Haystack Mountain

Soon, the water supply dam of the old State Sanatorium is crossed. A half hour of step-like ascents now begins. Moderately steep to steep slopes alternate with level stretches, which keeps you from tiring. The forest you are passing through is mature maple-beech hardwood.

At 3.0 m. (4.9 km.) rather steep climbing commences and, before long, you reach a rocky outlook. Painted lines take you on up to the wooded summit. A large grassy meadow provides an open wide vista to the east and south.

Walking downslope a short way, one can see Whiteface Mountain to the left, in the northeast. Big Burn Mountain is directly before you. To the southeast, the outline of Algonquin appears to be the largest mountain on the horizon. However, Mt. Marcy is to her left, looking smaller because it is further away. Most of the High Peaks can be seen.

Closer in, Scarface Mountain is to the right front, with 1980 Olympic Village at its right. Further south, Ampersand Mountain rises, distinctly separate from the more distant Seward Range at its left. On a clear day this has to be one of the most enjoyable views in the mountains.

A short walk northward through the spruces provides a lookout across the narrow valley to huge McKenzie Mountain. Both Haystack and McKenzie Mountains make good winter snowshoeing outings. Haystack is shorter by 3.0 m. (4.9 km.)

37. OWEN AND COPPERAS PONDS WALK
Round Trip Time—2 hrs.
Round Trip Distance—2.6 m. (4.1 km.)
Elevation Change—174 ft. (53 m.)
Difficulty—Easy with a few short grades.
Map—Lake Placid Quadrangle (1:125,000) or
    Lake Placid Quadrangle (1:25,000 metric)

A walk at Owen and Copperas Ponds can be a two hour interlude or a whole afternoon of relaxation in the midst of natural beauty. The route described here can be extended by a side trip to Winch Pond. If two vehicles are available, a loop route is possible by leaving the second car at the Copperas Pond trailhead, 1.0 m. (1.6 km.) north from where the Owen Pond trailhead is located on Rte. 86.

Access to the Owen Pond trailhead is on the east side of Rte. 86, approximately 5.0 m. (8.1 km.) northeast of the intersection of Rtes. 86 and 73 at Lake Placid. This is about 2.0 m. (3.2 km.) beyond the junction with River Road, which comes across from the Olympic Ski Jump on Rte. 73. There is parking for a few cars at the trailhead and also parking space on the opposite side of the road.

Blue DEC trail markers follow a tote road for about 420 ft. (129 m.). The trail then turns left from the tote road and continues along the right bank of Owen Pond Brook. A small grade brings you up to a hemlock grove. You hike far above the brook, looking down at its rippling flow. Owen Pond is reached at 0.6 m. (0.9 km.). Take the time to go to one of the side paths leading to its shoreline. One of the Sentinel Mountains stands out across the water at the far shore.

The path moves away from the pond, climbing a slope which alternately steepens and lessens. Swinging to the north, a junction is reached at the top of the grade. The pond is seen below and the trail descends steeply to it at the right. Copperas Pond lean-to No. 1 (placed on an ideal campsite) is reached at 1.3 m. (2.1 km.). An attractive picture emerges as one gazes across the pond. Great cliffs rise straight upward, with the crest of Whiteface Mountain soaring still higher beyond them as a backdrop. It is truly spectacular.

This short walk changes continuously as the seasons cast their special magic. Early spring flowers spatter the open woods floor. Young buds soon burst into leaves, drawing a veil over the forest. Shadows play their tricks and spiders weave their webs in the warming days of summer. Radiant leaves form a patchwork quilt, with conifers adding just the right amount of green, as autumn suddenly dashes in. Finally, the white snow of winter clears the easel until nature's artist begins afresh in the new year.

Soon after passing the lean-to, a trail right leads to Winch Pond. Bearing left, a second lean-to is found on the north shoreline. A path continues on around the pond edge to a nice picnic and swimming spot.

The second Rte. 86 trailhead is another 0.7 m. (1.2 km.) along the trail. A second branch trail to Winch Pond is reached shortly after you cross the bridge over Copperas Pond Outlet. Should you turn right here, you will reach Winch Pond after a short twenty minute side trip over a minor ridge. By bearing left at this junction, you proceed on toward Rte. 86.

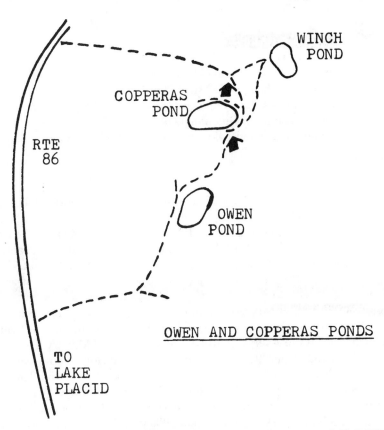

WINCH POND

COPPERAS POND

RTE 86

OWEN POND

OWEN AND COPPERAS PONDS

TO LAKE PLACID

Whiteface Mountain from Copperas Pond

38. WANIKA FALLS

Round Trip Time — 7 hrs.
Round Trip Distance — 13.4 m. (21.8 km.)
Elevation Change — 582 ft. (178 m.)
Difficulty — A very long trip over easy terrain.
Map — Santanoni Quadrangle or Saranac Lake
and Ampersand Lake Quadrangles (1:25,000 metric)

The Wanika Falls hike is a beautiful walk over the north end of the Northville-Placid Trail. The trip is longer than it used to be because of the rerouting of this section of trail in 1977. It is a long day's hike. The trail and falls are worth the effort, however. Endurance and time are factors for consideration. The actual terrain covered is not at all difficult.

Access to the trailhead is off the Averyville Road, south of Lake Placid. Averyville Road intersects Rte. 73 in the village of Lake Placid at the Newman Opera House. If approaching Lake Placid from Saranac Lake on Rte. 86, you may take the Old Military Road to the Northville-Placid Trail at the Averyville Road intersection. Old Military Road can also be reached from Rte. 73, near the Lake Placid Horse Show grounds. From the N-P sign at the Old Military Road intersection, drive 1.2 m. (1.9 km.) south on Averyville Road to the Chubb River bridge. A N-P sign indicates the trailhead and a small parking area at this point. A much larger and better parking area is found 900 ft. (275 m.) further down the road at the right.

The trail passes a DEC register and follows blue trail markers along a tote road beside Chubb River for 475 ft. (145 m.). Here, it branches left and becomes a foot path. Elevation is gradually gained. The route now crosses several tributaries and low divides as it generally progresses southward in a sweeping arc. The undulating course passes through a hardwood forest on a good trail for the next 1.2 m. (2.0 km.).

The next 1.1 m. (1.7 km.) has several soggy spots that must be crossed. They are somewhat dispersed and are of no consequence.

Once past this wet section, you reenter the hardwoods. The next 3.6 m. (5.8 km.) to Chubb River passes through some of the nicest forest in the Adirondacks. About half an hour after beginning this section, you cross a bridge and begin a long gradual climb on an old tote road. A gurgling brook is seen below you to the right. As you reach the top of the grade, the trail branches left, away from the tote road. Soon after, a rather large vlei comes into view on the right. Finally, about three hours after you began this trip, you descend a small grade and connect up with the old N-P Trail cutoff at Chubb River.

A rather bouncy bridge takes you over a high rocky section of the Chubb River. It might be well to walk upstream a short distance and rock hop across the water where it is much safer. Turning left from the bridge, the route takes you upstream beside the river. For 0.7 m. (1.1 km.) you steadily gain elevation until the water is far below you. The trail levels and you soon reach the trail junction for Wanika Falls. Were you to continue straight ahead for another 124.5 m. (201.7 km.) you would arrive at Northville on the Great Sacandaga Lake, having passed through one of the most remote parts of the Adirondacks.

Turn left and proceed about 500 ft. (153 m.) up the steep trail to the Wanika Falls lean-to. Some falls are seen here, but the really spectacular falls are found about 100 yds. (92 m.) upstream from the lean-to. Here, in a series of drops, water cascades several hundred feet to a pool. It is not only beautiful but beckons you to a refreshing swim before lunch.

39. MT. JO

Round Trip Time—1 hr. and 45 min.
Round Trip Distance—2.3 m. (3.7 km.)
Elevation Change—710 ft. (217 m.)
Summit Elevation—2876 ft. (880 m.)
Difficulty—An easy mountain because of its
     short distance, but steep in places.
Map—Mt. Marcy Quadrangle

Mt. Jo is a special mountain. In 1877, Henry Van Hoevenberg and his fiancee Josephine Scofield climbed Mt. Marcy, their intent being to choose from all they surveyed the place for their future home. A tiny heart-shaped lake, far to the north, was selected. The mountain near it was named Mt. Jo, after Josephine. Then tragedy struck. Josephine died within a year. She was never to see her home completed. But Van Hoevenberg carried on and completed the well known Adirondack Lodge, which was later destroyed by the great forest fire in 1903. Some years later the Lake Placid Club acquired the property, rebuilding the inn. Melville Dewey, a driving force behind the reconstruction and a proponent of phonetic spelling, provided his own inimitable mark of peculiar spelling. Today the complex is known as Adirondak Loj and is owned and operated by the Adirondack Mountain Club. Tender memories of a time forever lost linger on this tiny mountain top.

Mt. Jo is on the Adirondak Loj property at Heart Lake. It is reached via Heart Lake Road by turning off Rte. 73 at the DEC "Trail to the High Peaks" sign. This is 4.0 m. (6.5 km.) southeast of the village of Lake Placid. At 4.8 m. (7.8 km.) down Heart Lake Road, turn left into the public parking area at the Campers and Hikers Building.

From the entrance of the parking area, walk 500 ft. (153 m.) back down Heart Lake Road to the Indian Pass trail on the left. Follow this trail a short distance, turning right when a T-junction is reached. You soon cross a small bridge. The Mt. Jo trail begins on the right, immediately beyond the bridge.

The trail is well marked with blue paint blazes and ADK markers on small stakes. Leaving the Indian Pass trail, the route immediately turns left and climbs to the junction of the Long and Short summit trails. To make a loop trip, the Long Trail is described for the ascent and the Short Trail is described for the descent.

The Long Trail bears left and gradually circles the base of the mountain, with little change of elevation. At 0.6 m. (1.0 km.), a sharp pitch begins your real climbing. At 1.0 m. (1.6 km.), the Short Trail rejoins the Long Trail. From here, the remainder of the trip is easy, with a little rock climbing just before reaching the summit.

Splendid views are found from Mt. Jo. Heart Lake is seen below. Looking southward, the MacIntyre Range of Wright Peak, Algonquin, Boundary, Iroquois, and Marshall opens up. Slightly to the left, over Mt. Colden, Mt. Marcy can be seen. Further left, over Phelps, the Great Range comes into view. Whiteface Mountain can be seen in the northwest. All in all, this is a very fine observation point for such a short climb.

The return route is the reverse of the ascent until the junction with the Short Trail is reached. The Short Trail branches left. It is quite steep but has some rather unusual rock formations along the way. It does require a bit of agile footwork, in places, since some of the trail is heavily eroded. However, a number of outlooks make the paint-marked trail interesting.

CRANBERRY LAKE, WANAKENA,
AND WEST SECTION

The Cranberry Lake, Wanakena, and West Section is a relatively isolated area. The old ways still linger here. The people have a pride and friendliness that clearly tell you how much they enjoy this country.

Frederic Remington understood this when he summered at Witch's Bay on Cranberry Lake. The feelings of many are expressed near the mouth of Sucker Brook on this same lake. There, chiseled into the Reuben Wood Rock, are words in commemoration of a world champion fly casting champion of yesteryear. "In memory of Reuben Wood, a genial gentleman and great fisherman who was fond of these solitudes." Many are drawn to these solitudes.

The river people along the St. Lawrence have passed Sunday Rock for years on their way to the "South Woods." It took the automobile, however, to open the way into this region from other directions. Even the rivers flow northward, away from the larger cities of the state. Now, campers from Syracuse, Rochester, and Watertown frequent the area.

For flatland hiking in an exceptional setting, this is a marvelous section of the Adirondacks. The hiker who also likes to paddle a canoe will find no finer place to combine the two pleasures.

Access to this section is by Rtes. 3, 56 and 58. Towns are far apart and traffic is light. Be sure your vehicle is in proper running condition.

Sunday Rock. Four-tenths of a mile (0.6 km.) north of the Raquette River bridge in the town of South Colton a dull grey boulder is found. It used to sit along the dusty road traveled by vacationers in their wagons as they headed for the "South Woods" from the Canton area. Natives have long known it as Sunday Rock.

It doesn't appear unique. As boulders go, it is rather modest in size, though a bit more regular in shape than most. Its significance is not in substance, but in what it represents.

For some reason, this rock always caught the eye of the tired traveler on his way to a place of revitalization. It was said there was no Sunday beyond this rock. Once past this point, one entered a world of timelessness, where one was freed of the restrictions of more formal society. A special land was entered here.

When the automobile came along, the narrow road had to be widened. Sunday Rock was in the way. A hue and cry arose throughout the North Country. The Sunday Rock Association was formed to save it. First, the *Watertown Daily Times* and later the *Brooklyn Eagle* took up the banner.

Public opinion eventually prevailed. The rock was carefully removed from its position and today sits in its little park with dignity and respect.

The whole thing was a sentimental gesture, but those who love the Adirondacks are that way. They know Sunday Rock represents the spirit that draws them to these woods. Though the physical beauty of this land is immense, it is really the sense of unencumbered freedom in the midst of this beauty that is unique here. This ageless boulder symbolizes man's determination that the essence of the Adirondacks shall always survive.

Sunday Rock at South Colton

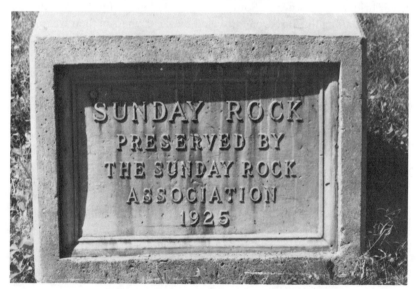

40. CAT MOUNTAIN

Round Trip Time—5 hrs.
Round Trip Distance—11.2 m. (18.1 km.)
Elevation Change—766 ft. (234 m.)
Summit Elevation—2261 ft. (691 m.)
Difficulty—Easy, but a fairly long trip.
Map—Cranberry Lake Quadrangle

This trail is part of an immense hiking system into one of the finest wilderness areas of the Adirondacks. Extended trips of over a week are possible in this region.

Access to the trailhead is from the village of Wanakena. Wanakena is 1 m. (1.6 km.) off Rte. 3. As you proceed to Wanakena, bear right at any road forks you come to. After you cross the Oswegatchie River on a one-lane metal bridge, travel 0.5 m. (0.8 km.) until you reach a small DEC sign indicating the Dead Creek Flow fire road. There is a parking area just past the gated fire road.

Follow the fire road 2.0 m. (3.2 km.) to its end. The almost level grassy lane passes through a most interesting deciduous forest. After about twenty-five minutes of walking, you pass a pretty little vlei on the right. Five minutes later, you catch your first glimpse of Dead Creek Flow on the left. The fire road then parallels the flow until you reach its terminus. Here, you'll find a picnic table and a fireplace. Janack's Landing can be seen across the water.

The trail, now a path, continues on another 1.1 m (1.8 km.) to another trail junction. On the way, Dead Creek and a second brook are crossed on log bridges. From the junction, Janack's Landing is 0.2 m. (0.3 km.) to the left. This makes a good swimming spot on the return trip.

Bearing right, red markers lead you on a flat trail for some fifteen minutes. Then you very gradually gain elevation as you pass through a draw. Approaching the end of the draw, the trail becomes a moderately steep grade for a short distance.

Just beyond the height of land, you again come to a trail junction. The blue Plains Trail goes straight on down the slope ahead. You should stay on the red trail, which bears left along the ridge.

Moving on, the sound of rushing water is soon heard. Before long, you reach the cascading waters of Glasby Pond Outlet. The trail follows the outlet a short half mile (0.8 km.) to Glasby Pond. A pretty fern meadow is passed through just before you reach the pond. At the pond's edge you cross the outlet on a log bridge. Glasby Pond is a jewel. Its dark water is surrounded by bushes, giving it a primitive look.

The red trail soon bears right and for some distance is above the water level. This provides a splendid view of the pond and the mountain beyond.

Leaving the pond, the trail begins to climb gradually, until a trail junction is reached. The yellow trail to the right leads to Cowhorn Junction. Continue straight ahead for Cat Mountain.

Cat Mountain Pond from Cat Mountain

The summit is only 0.6 m. (0.8 km.) ahead. The trail is moderate and levels frequently. Eventually you run straight into a very high massive bluff. The only real climbing occurs here as you climb a very steep one hundred vertical feet up a narrow rock path.

At the top the trail swings right, passes a couple lookouts, and soon reaches the summit. Only the foundation of the fire tower remains, but you have a splendid view from the open rock. As you move around the rock bluff to the left, charming vistas appear to the east, where the high peaks are seen in the far distance. Cat Mt. Pond is seen below.

As your eyes sweep the vast forest region, it is hard to believe that all this was desolation in 1908, when sparks from locomotives started fires that devastated this region. The recuperative power of nature is great, but let's hope that man has not forgotten this terrible lesson from our past.

41. HIGH FALLS

Round Trip Time—5 hrs. 30 min.
Round Trip Distance—12.8 m. (20.7 km.)
Elevation Change—123 ft. (38 m.)
Difficulty—Easy walking, but a long trip.
Map—Cranberry Lake Quadrangle

High Falls is a cataract on the Oswegatchie River, where the flow squeezes through a narrow channel in the rock and jets out in a burst of white foam. Cascading downward, its cooling spray sets up breezes that make this a tremendously pleasant place to be on a hot summer day.

Access to the trailhead is from the village of Wanakena. Wanakena is 1.0 m. (1.6 km.) off Rte. 3. As you proceed to Wanakena, bear right at any road forks you come to. When you cross the Oswegatchie River on a one lane metal bridge, take care. At 0.1 m. (0.2 km.) beyond the bridge on the right is a small sign pointing down the High Falls truck road. There is a metal gate a few hundred feet along this road. The trail begins there.

Parking is available on the right side of the paved road, just beyond the tennis courts and past the turn-off for the truck road. Parking also is available for a small fee at the private home just before the truck trail gate.

The first part of the DEC red marked trail is perfectly flat and open. A narrow pond on the left is passed. Finally, you begin to climb gradually upward as you enter the woods. Below on the right Skate Creek can be seen. The trail becomes quite rocky and the junction with the Leary Trail is reached at 1.8 m. (2.9 km.).

Follow the blue marked trail which branches left and proceeds up a fair grade. Over the next 3.0 m. (4.9 km.) the trail moderately rises and drops frequently as it takes you through a deciduous forest. A few swampy areas and streams are crossed. Beaver activity may cause minor walking difficulty just before the trail emerges out of the forest onto the truck trail again.

Leave the blue trail you have been following. It continues straight on into the distant Five Ponds Wilderness Area. You should turn left and follow the red marked truck trail. High Falls is another 1.6 m. (2.6 km.).

This portion of the truck trail is both easier to walk on and more interesting in its surroundings. The soil is sandier. Tamarack trees, the only deciduous conifers, are seen in this section. Their delicate stringy boughs are easily spotted.

About a mile (1.6 km.) down this road the Plains Trail comes in from the left. If time permits on the return trip, you might walk in a way on this trail. It is a most unique place. The extensive open region of berry bushes and flowers doesn't seem to grow in with trees. It is thought that extreme variations in yearly groundwater levels might be the reason. On any account, a walk through the Plains is a most unforgettable experience.

Eight-tenths of a mile (1.3 km.) further on you'll arrive at High Falls. A lean-to is found on each side of the river. An attractive wooden bridge crosses the stream above the falls. Deep pools invite you to swim. Enjoy yourself.

High Falls on Oswegatchie River

42. THE MOORE TRAIL

Round Trip Time—2 hrs.
Round Trip Distance—4 m. (6.5 km.)
Elevation Change—Negligible
Difficulty—Easy.
Map—Cranberry Lake Quadrangle

View from the Moore Trail

The Moore Trail is a pretty walk along the north shoreline of the Oswegatchie River from Wanakena to Inlet.

Access to the trailhead is from the village of Wanakena. Wanakena is 1.0 m. (1.6 km.) off Rte. 3. As you proceed to Wanakena, bear right at any forks you come to. Just before the single lane metal bridge across the Oswegatchie River, you notice a small DEC sign attached to a tree on the right. It indicates the direction to Inlet and is marked 2.0 m. (3.2 km.). This is the Moore Trail. You may park your car off the road at this point. The wide grassy lane for canoe access leads directly to the stream. A short distance along this way, you'll notice a narrow trail to the right through the tall grass. Follow this. It very soon becomes a wide and pretty woods trail, along the river.

The trail is essentially level, except for a few places where it briefly rises a few feet above water level. It follows the stream to Inlet. This section of the river moves rapidly and has many rocks. It is not passable by canoeists unless they are white water experts. Even then some portages are required.

On a summer day, the trail provides a pleasant respite for the traveler. Many places beckon you to sit at the shoreline to watch the surging water. Its constant roar masks most other sounds and is relaxing. It is an excellent place to practice photography.

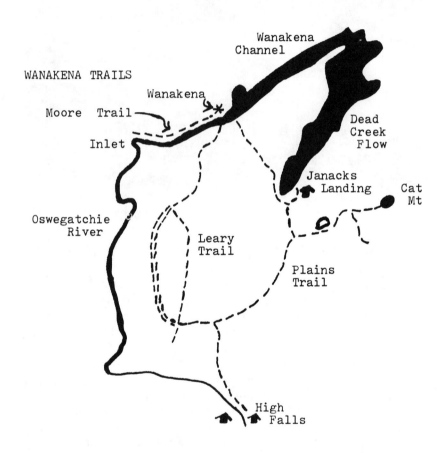

43. BEAR MOUNTAIN

Round Trip Time — 2 hrs.
Round Trip Distance — 3.6 m. (5.8 km.)
Elevation Change — 742 ft. (227 m.)
Summit Elevation — 2242 ft. (686 m.)
Difficulty — Easy, with a few steep places.
Map — Cranberry Lake Quadrangle

Bear Mountain is on the north shore of Cranberry Lake. It offers a pretty view of the lake. Short enough so that swimming and picnicking can be combined with the climb, it makes a nice little outing.

Access to the trailhead is off Rte. 3 at the Cranberry Lake Public Campsite and Picnic Area. This is just east of the village of Cranberry Lake. Turning at the large sign, drive 1.2 m. (1.9 km.) until you come to the park's toll booth. There is a small day use charge for entering the park. Proceed past the picnic and beach area until at 0.5 m. (0.8 km.) you reach the DEC sign for Bear Mountain. There is a large parking area at the left.

The trail leaves the right rear of the parking area where there is a trail register. Follow red DEC markers. The almost level trail passes through a predominantly beech forest. Quite rocky at first, it becomes more comfortable as elevation is gained.

Two small brooks are crossed. At 0.6 m. (1.0 km.) the grade becomes moderately steep and steadily climbs for a few moments. A short distance from where the trail briefly levels again a lean-to is passed on the left.

After crossing a small brook on a log bridge, climbing again becomes moderate to moderately steep. Soon the trail swings up to the left and steepens considerably. This is the only really steep part of the trail. You soon reach the top of the mountain ridge and proceed along the flat summit for about ten minutes.

Here the forest is more open and the trees are somewhat smaller. You actually are slowly losing some elevation. Passing between two immense boulders, you enter an interesting boulder field. Strewn about like so many checkers, the many boulders in this location were dropped by the last glaciers about ten thousand years ago.

The easy walking continues, until at 1.5 m. (2.4 km.) you reach the lookout. From this point you look directly down on Joe Indian Island in Cranberry Lake. To the left is Buck Island. Beyond it at Barber's Point is the Cranberry Lake Biological Station. Run by the forestry school of Syracuse University, it provides remarkable training for our future foresters. Just to the right of Joe Indian Island, Dead Creek Flow and the Wanakena Channel begin.

In 1908, fire swept this mountain top. Still earlier, a hunter who was stung by hornets got even by burning their nest and half of the mountain. He was smart enough to keep that a secret for many years.

A loop can be made by continuing along the ridge. It is a very nice trail for 0.9 m. (1.5 km.), but it does mean 1.0 m. (1.6 km.) of walking the paved road back through the park to your starting point after you leave the forest.

Still following the red DEC markers, the trail follows the ridge for a few minutes. Then it rather steeply descends for about five minutes. Moderating, the trail continues through a nice hardwood forest. A very large rock outcrop is passed on the right, at 2.4 m. (3.4 km.). Finally the lake is seen ahead through the trees. Crossing a small tributary of the lake on a rustic bridge, you reach the paved road.

Turn right and follow this road to the first junction. Turn right again and stay on this road until you reach the parking area where you left your vehicle. It will take about twenty minutes of walking to cover this distance.

44. ARAB MOUNTAIN

Round Trip Time — 1 hr. 30 min.
Round Trip Distance — 2.1 m. (3.4 km.)
Elevation Change — 760 ft. (232 m)
Summit Elevation — 2545 ft. (778 m.)
Difficulty — Easy, with varying grades.
Map — Tupper Lake Quadrangle

Geographically, this mountain sits like a large strawberry at the bottom of an enormous flattened bowl, waiting to provide a delicious dessert for the hiker. Though not great in elevation, it is higher than its immediate surroundings. Thus there are excellent views in all directions from its summit.

Access to the trailhead is off Rte. 3. Between the hamlets of Gale and Piercefield, turn south at the sign for Conifer. At 1.7 m. (2.8 km.) there is a left turn. A large sign points the way to Eagle Crag Lake. A smaller DEC sign indicates it is 1.7 m. (2.8 km.) to Mt. Arab. It is, but that includes the walking. The trailhead is actually only 0.9 m. (1.5 km.) further. A railroad track is crossed 0.3 m. (0.5 km.) before the small DEC sign indicating the trailhead is reached. It is on the left side of the road. Parking is available for several cars on the opposite side of the road.

Red DEC markers lead the way through a beech-maple forest. A well designed new trail has replaced the older one. The two criss-cross each other frequently, but just follow the red markers. The trail rises slowly, leveling off frequently.

At 0.4 m. (0.6 km.) a sign is reached indicating a spring located to the left. Yellow painted tree blazes take one down the slope some distance to the spring.

Soon after, the trail becomes moderately steep. It turns left at a large boulder. Reaching the ridge line at 0.6 m. (1.0 km.), the now nearly level path leads through a pretty maple and red spruce growth. It is quite pleasant after the climbing you've just completed. Two rock outcrops are passed. The trail swings to the right around the second of these. One last rise brings you to the fire observer's cabin and the fire tower. The true summit is slightly further on, beyond a small col, but the described trail terminates at the tower.

The summit is relatively flat. It is a floral bouquet bordered by berry bushes. To the west is Tupper Lake. Beyond the lake are the High Peaks. There is a 360-degree panorama. Mt. Arab Lake and Eagle Crag Lake are below to the southeast. To the north Mt. Matumbla and St. Regis Mountain are found. The rim of the horizon is full of mountain ridges.

The grades found on this trail are ideal for snowshoeing. The reward for a sunny winter's tramp to this summit would be great for such a short climb.

THE NORTH—NORTHEAST SECTION

The North—Northeast Section has a somewhat different character from the rest of the Adirondacks. Lake Champlain dominates. The French influence is felt in its people and in the names of such places as the Ausable and Bouquet rivers. The heyday of this region was founded on the steamboat, the railroad, and the stagecoach.

Ausable Forks was a primary point of embarkation for stages heading into the high peaks. At one time, the Franklin House in Franklin Falls counted well over a thousand guests each season. This was the gateway to the mountains, until the automobile changed travel patterns of vacationers. Now both the stagecoach and the Franklin House have disappeared from this region.

The North—Northeast Section has quietly withdrawn from the spotlight, but it still retains its own charm. There is great history here. It is indeed an interesting place for the hiker who realizes that a knowledge of the past greatly enhances the appreciation of the present. Access to this section is via Rte. 87 (Adirondack Northway) and Rtes. 30, 72, 3 and 9.

45. POKE-O-MOONSHINE MOUNTAIN
Round Trip Time—2 hrs. 30 min.
Round Trip Distance—2.4 m. (3.9 km.)
Elevation Change—1280 ft. (391 m.)
Summit Elevation—2180 ft. (667 m.)
Difficulty—A short hike, with some steep sections.
Map—Ausable Forks Quadrangle

The historian Beauchamp believed the unusual name Poke-O-Moonshine was derived from the Algonquin words "Pohquis" (it is broken) and "Moosie" (smooth). "Pohquis-Moosie" described the sheer cliffs found on this mountain. Others feel the name simply refers to the haunting glens and supposed spirits of this peak. Whatever the facts, this climb rewards the hiker with outstanding views of Lake Champlain to the east and the High Peaks to the southwest. In season, a profusion of ferns borders the hiking trail near the summit.

The trail begins at the south end of the Poke-O-Moonshine State Campsite along Rte. 9. This is about 12 m. (19.4 km.) north of Elizabethtown and 7 m. (11.3 km.) south from Keeseville. If driving north on Rte. 87, exit at Interchange 32 and drive west to Rte. 9. Then take Rte. 9 north 9 m. (15 km.) to the campsite. If driving south on Rte. 87, exit at Interchange 33. Drive a short distance to Rte. 9 and then proceed southward about 3 m. (3.9 km.) to the campsite.

The red-marked DEC trail begins at the south end of the campsite. A small day-use fee will be levied for parking.

Soon the route steepens. A very high rock formation is reached. Bypassing it to the left, outlooks are reached after a few more minutes. The last outlook has a bench-shaped boulder that appears to have been put there especially for hikers to rest on.

The difficulty in climbing varies considerably over the next half mile (0.8 km.). The glen containing the remains of the fire observer's cabin provides welcome respite. It is quite picturesque. A lean-to is found on a side trail to the left of the cabin, some 65 yds. (60 m.) away. A tote road beyond the lean-to has many blueberries. This is a good place to rest before the final burst to the summit.

There are two ways to the top from the cabin. The short way makes a sharp right turn from the cabin. It leads steeply up the old eroded trail to the tower. An enclosed spring is found a few yards along this route.

The easier and now official route follows red trail markers from the right rear of the cabin. It circles the summit, gradually reaching the fire tower. Many bare ledges are passed along the way. The bare rock summit and its fire tower offer a striking panorama. To the east a sweeping view of Lake Champlain, some 8 m. (13 km.) away, stands out. The Green Mountains of Vermont form a backdrop. Mansfield and Camel's Hump are clearly seen. To the south is Deerfield Mountain, with the Jays behind it. To its left is Hurricane Mountain. Distant Gothics is on Hurricane's right shoulder. To the left of Hurricane Mountain is Giant. Right of Deerfield Mountain is the Sentinel Range, twenty miles away. Whiteface Mountain is almost due west. Lyon Mountain is due north, beyond Baldface,

Looking south from Poke-O-Moonshine

which is further down the ridge. On a clear day, Mt. Royal, ninety miles off in Montreal, can be seen. The hiker who has the time can spend it well by hiking along the crest of this mountain.

Colvin surveyed from this mountain in the 1870's. The careful searcher may locate a copper bolt, marked 26. It indicates this was Station 26 of the survey.

46. LYON MOUNTAIN
Round Trip Time—3 hrs. 30 min.
Round Trip Distance—5.0 m. (8.1 km.)
Elevation Change—1790 ft. (547 m.)
Summit Elevation—3830 ft. (1171 m.)
Difficulty—Steep for much of the climb, a
**   rigorous High Peak-type trail.**
Map—Lyon Mountain Quadrangle

Charles Merril was only eighteen in the spring of 1881 when his father sent him up Lyon Mountain. What was unusual was that he didn't come down for two weeks. The Rev. Thomas Cook of Troy was suffering from asthma, and it was felt the high elevation might help him. It did. Young Merril was his guide. Dozens of mountains could be seen in all directions. On June 20, 1881, a roaring hail and snow storm took them by surprise. It was an exciting adventure, and Merril never forgot it. He continued on and became a well-known Adirondack guide for many years.

Access to the trailhead is off Chazy Lake Road on the southwest shore of the lake. This can be reached from Rte. 3, starting at the Chazy Lake Road sign for Lyon Mountain Village at Pickett's Corners. After passing a crossroads, turn left at the T-intersection 0.6 m. (1.0 km.) from Rte. 3. This is County Rte. 8. Continuing along, your route turns right at a crossroads after another 1.9 m. (3.1 km.). You then proceed, still on Rte. 8, for another 5.7 m. (9.2 km.).

Here there is a gravel road at the left. Near its entrance once stood a large double-posted sign which indicated the entry road to the former Lowenberg Ski Area. If you are approaching on Rte. 374 from Dannemora, this gravel road would be 1.8 m. (2.9 km.) south from where you pick up Rte. 8.

Proceed along this wide gravel road for 0.9 m. (1.5 km.) until you reach the ruins of the ski lodge. A large parking area is at this point. Distances in the description from this point on are estimated.

On the left side of the lodge is a hardscrabble road. It is grown in at its beginning but soon opens up. Gradually climbing, you follow this road for about a mile (1.6 km.). You can see the fire tower occasionally as you walk along.

After about half an hour the road swings abruptly to the right, but your trail continues straight ahead into the woods. A small stream is soon crossed. The trail now becomes moderately steep. It will remain so for another twenty-five minutes.

The telephone wires you have been following bring you to a small sloped clearing, where you will find the fire observer's cabin and a few outbuildings. There is a brook to the left of the cabin. The trail also goes to the left. It would be well to take a long drink and rest here before tackling the next stretch.

The way steepens considerably for the next three quarters of a mile (1.2 km.). It is rocky and you must watch your footing. Eventually, you'll notice a small bench at a turn in the trail. An outlook is on the right and the trail goes to the left.

From this point, the path almost levels. It takes you through a nice spruce stand. Ten minutes later the tower is before you. The rocky summit has good views. On a clear day the glittering spires of Notre Dame Cathedral in Montreal may be seen. Mt. Marcy and the High Peaks are to the south. Northeast of you, Chazy Lake stretches forth. Upper and Lower Chateaugay Lakes are west. By careful observation, it is possible to trace the flow of the Saranac River almost all the way to Lake Champlain.

47. TAYLOR POND PRIMITIVE CAMPING AREA
Map — Lyon Mountain Quadrangle

Taylor Pond Primitive Campsite

113

A primitive camping area is a place where camping is permitted but where facilities are kept to a minimum. Unlike the state's public campsites (state parks), there are no showers, lifeguards, paved roads, etc. On the other hand, there is a ranger near and a few other people.

Taylor Pond is located along the Clayburg-Ausable Forks road. It is approximately 2 m. (3.2 km.) east of the Union Falls Road, near Silver Lake. For the beginner, it offers a chance to test out-of-door skills in a relatively safe atmosphere. For the experienced camper, it is a chance to enjoy the out-of-doors without the usual hardships. There are day use and overnight camping fees.

The Taylor Pond area is truly a beautiful place, looking out towards Catamount Mountain. Over 14 m. (22.7 km.) of trails circuit the body of water. Originally developed as snowmobile trails, they are now receiving considerable winter use by cross-country skiers. In the summer they make excellent flatland hiking, often bordering the water. Day trips can be planned to meet the capabilities of the hikers.

The three lean-tos on the pond can best be reached by canoe. A few other sandy beach areas are suitable for camping.

Taylor Pond makes a good base area for more rigorous mountain activities. Catamount Mountain is just across the lake. Duncan Mountain is not far. The Silver Lake Mountain trail is again open for use.

This type of setting is fine for family and other small group activities. The beginner who is hesitant to plunge into the forest for the first time may well find the primitive camping area is the happy middle ground.

Stump at Taylor Pond

48. AZURE MOUNTAIN (BLUE MOUNTAIN)
Round Trip Time—1 hr. 30 min.
Round Trip Distance—1.0 m. (1.6 km.)
Elevation Change—Estimated 700 ft. (214 m.)
Summit Elevation—2518 ft. (770 m.)
Difficulty—Easy, with some steep spots.
Map—Santa Clara Quadrangle

Another of the outpost mountains, Azure Mountain provides a simply magnificent view of the distant High Peaks from the north. This is in sharp contrast to the numerous small bodies of water found at its base. Altogether one earns a striking picture from climbing this small peak. Access to the trailhead is off Rte. 458, 4 m. (6.5 km.) south of St. Regis Falls or about 3 m. (4.9 km.) north of Santa Clara. At this point, Blue Mountain Road is reached on the south side of the road. It is directly opposite the Blue Mountain Inn. Blue Mountain Road is a broad gravel road in excellent condition.

Following Blue Mountain Road for 6.7 m. (10.9 km.), a sign indicating a spring on state land is seen at the right. Fill your canteens here, since there is no water on the mountain. Further on 0.4 m. (0.6 km.), a small road is reached on the right.

This narrow dirt road leads 0.1 m. (0.2 km.) to a gate and trailhead. The trail leads another 0.3 m. (0.5 km.) to a fire observer's cabin.

The trail passes between the cabin and its outbuildings. (This used to be the starting point of the hike before the gate was installed.) As you climb, note the changing tree types as subtle ecological conditions occur.

Entering a mature maple forest, the first few hundred feet of path rise gradually. Almost all of the rest of the trail, however, varies from moderately steep to steep. It is a short but rigorous climb. The trail is marked with both red DEC markers and yellow paint blazes. To ease the ascent, numerous switchbacks have been designed into the trail. For your walking safety and to prevent erosion of the mountain, follow the official trail. Do not use the goat paths that follow the telephone wires. At 0.2 m. (0.3 km.) a small sign on the right points the way to a switchback around a particularly steep spot.

The trail moderates for the last few hundred feet. The tower is soon seen ahead. Walking through high brush and long grass, you are at the tower before you can see far into the distance.

Beyond the tower open rock provides a panorama that is exquisite. Below you are numerous ponds. The deep blue bodies of water seem to be surrounded by a hundred shades of green, such is the variation in vegetation.

Out to the south is Whiteface Mountain, Giant, the Great Range, Marcy, the McIntyres, and the Sewards. Closer in are dozens of lesser ridges. Huge Debar Mountain stands out in the east. The thin ribbon of water to the north is the St. Lawrence River.

The huge boulder on the edge of the drop-off on the west side of the open rock is another of nature's mysteries. Just why did the glaciers of the last ice age choose that spot to leave such a giant rock? Perhaps it is to remind us of the great power of their forces.

View from Azure Mountain

49. DEBAR MOUNTAIN

Round Trip Time — 4 hrs. 30 min.
Round Trip Distance — 7.3 m. (11.9 km.)
Elevation Change — 1,726 ft. (528 m.)
Summit Elevation — 3,300 ft. (1,009 m.)
Difficulty — Generally easy, but the last half mile
   is as steep as anything in the Adirondacks that
   has a trail.
Map — Loon Lake and Santa Clara Quadrangles

Far to the north, Debar Mountain sits beside beautiful Meacham Lake. Surrounded by state forests, she is isolated. Climbing 800 ft. (245 m.) in the last 0.5 m. (0.8 km.), the peak offers a mixture of easy woods walking and rugged climbing. Plan to make use of the wonderful beach while at Meacham Lake.

Access to the mountain trail is from Rte. 30 at Meacham Lake Public Campsite. This is 18 m. (29.2 km.) south of Malone. It is 2.4 m. (3.9 km.) from the Rte. 30 park sign to the toll booth at the park. A small day use charge is required before entering the campsite.

Proceed straight ahead from the toll booth 0.2 m. (0.3 km.) until you see a small sign on the left indicating the turn for Debar Mountain. This is the left hand turn for campsites 21-52. Just past campsite 48, bear right onto the sandy road which branches off. At 0.4 m. (0.6 km.) along this road, you'll arrive at a large parking area and the gate which marks the beginning of the trail.

Red trail markers take you along a woods road through a mixed forest occasionally heavy with balsam fir. The way is almost flat in this section. At 0.8 m. (1.3 km.) bear right at the fork in the road. Then, at 0.9 m. (1.5 km.), turn left at the junction. A small Debar Mountain Trail sign, high in a tree, points the way.

From here onward the grade varies from gradual to moderately steep. In general, it steepens gradually as you progress. At 2.3 m. (3.8 km.) it would appear the trail will take you right into a boulder. However, it swings to the left and continues on to a height of land at 2.5 m. (4.0 km.).

The following short level stretch ends and the trail descends slightly to a small creek. It then resumes its gradual upgrade course. A lean-to, on the left, is passed at 2.9 m. (4.7 km.). Your objective can be seen to the right front from this location. Soon after, the remains of the burnt-out fire observer's cabin are reached. Its small clearing is growing in from disuse.

The long walk to this point has been relatively easy. From here on, care must be taken. The trail narrows and becomes a rocky path. Before long the way becomes very steep, and it is frequently necessary to use your hands to get over some of the rocks. Eventually the trail moderates, and for the last five minutes you can catch your breath as you stride through a sweet-smelling stand of balsam fir.

Circling the base of the bald rock holding the fire tower, you finally reach the small, open, and rocky summit. The tower is not in good condition and should not be climbed.

Meacham Lake dominates the scene. Clear Pond is to its right. Far to the right is Deer River Flow. The High Peaks are to your extreme left, in the southeast. Whiteface, St. Regis, Morris, and Ampersand Mountains can be spotted. Around to the north are found Azure and Loon Lake Mountains and Lyon Mountain.

Portions of the trail and much of the park seem ideal for cross-country skiing. The upper stretches of the trail would require some mountain skiing skill and perhaps would be best done on snowshoes. Only those with considerable experience should try to snowshoe beyond the lean-to, however.

50. ST. REGIS MOUNTAIN
Round Trip Time — 3 hrs. 30 min.
Round Trip Distance — 4.9 m. (7.9 km.)
Elevation Change — 1,253 ft. (383 m.)
Summit Elevation — 2873 ft. (879 m.)
Difficulty — Generally moderate, but rather steep for last part.
Map — St. Regis Quadrangle

St. Regis Mountain stands alone, literally surrounded by over one hundred bodies of water. The sight of these rivers, ponds, and lakes from the summit is unmatched in the Adirondacks. To the southeast, most of the High Peaks can be seen on the horizon. This peak is worth scaling.

Access to the trailhead is from Keese Mills Road, near the intersection of Rtes. 30 and 192 at Paul Smiths. Drive down Keese Mills Road 2.6 m. (4.2 km.). At that point, a small DEC sign for St. Regis Mountain points the way to the left at an easily missed intersection. This is just past the Canoe Carry Parking Area for Black Pond. A narrow paved road leads 0.5 m. (0.8 km.) southward to the state's locked gate across the road. At the right is a large parking area and the trail sign.

The first 0.7 m. (1.1 km.) of the red DEC marked trail climbs over two small ridges having moderately steep grades. Take the left fork just past the top of the first ridge. Descending the second ridge, a metal link fence is reached and then followed for a short distance. Crossing a dirt road, you come to what used to be the trailhead. The quality of the trail greatly improves from this point onward.

The trail levels for the next five minutes. Two swampy creeks are traversed on wooden bridges. A long moderate grade takes you along the telephone line toward the summit. This is a very nice section of trail.

About forty-five minutes after your start, you pass a small cabin on the right, a stream, and then the fire observer's cabin, which is up on a slope to the left. The stream is the last sure water. The grade now increases slightly but is still very moderate.

Log steps are reached at 1.8 m. (2.9 km.). A sign points to the left, up a moderately steep to steep grade. The slope soon moderates again until another sign is reached fifteen minutes later.

Here, the new trail rises steeply to the right front. The older, now abandoned trail branches off to the right at a more gentle grade. The newer route is shorter but climbs 775 vertical ft. (237 m.) in the next 0.4 m. (0.6 km.).

You will finally break out of the trees onto the open rock near the summit. Flowers and shrubs abound. Views open to the east, behind you. The fire tower and register are soon reached.

Over-zealous survey crews burned off the top of St. Regis Mountain back in 1876. The bare summit offers unrestricted views in all directions. The myriad ponds and lakes are impossible to describe in detail. Upper St. Regis Lake and Spitfire Lake are due east. Lake Clear, Little Clear Pond, St. Regis Pond, and Hoel Pond are the close-by bodies of water to the south. Further south, Upper Saranac Lake stretches out into the distance. Whiteface Mountain lies 21 m. (34 km.) away, in line with Upper St. Regis Lake. Loon Lake Mountain stands out in the northeast, beyond Black Pond. Sable and Baldface Mountains separate it from the huge bulk of Debar Mountain to its left. Far in the southwest, Mt. Morris is seen to the left of Tupper Lake. The whole of the High Peaks are to the southeast. Marcy is seen in line with the right edge of Lake Clear on the horizon. Big Slide Mountain is over the center of Clear Pond. The rest of the High Peaks can be picked out and identified.

This would seem to be an absolutely perfect mountain to snowshoe on in the winter. The grades are moderate, except at the end. All but the summit is protected from the wind by trees.

Glossary

Bushwhack To make one's way through bushes or undergrowth.

Cairn A pile of stones set up to mark a summit or route.

Col A pass between two adjacent peaks.

Corduroy A road, trail or bridge formed by logs laid side by side transversely to facilitate crossing swampy places.

Duff Partly decayed vegetable matter on the forest floor.

Hardscrabble A very rough dirt road made up largely of rocks and small stones.

Lean-to An open camp with overhanging roof on the open side.

Massif A large, rocky prominence.

Paint Blazes Trail indicators painted on trees or rocks.

Tote Road An inferior road used for hauling, such as a lumber road, often with corduroys.

Vlei A marsh or swampy meadow (pronounced *vly*).

INDEX

Listings are entered by proper name first. Words like mount, mountain, lake, etc. follow the proper name.

122

INDEX of PEOPLE

Notes

Notes

**Other Publications
of
The Adirondack Mountain Club, Inc.
R.R. 3, Box 3055
Lake George, NY 12845-9523
(518) 668-4447**

AN ADIRONDACK SAMPLER II, Backpacking Trips
25 trips throughout the Park for novice and expert
GUIDE TO ADIRONDACK TRAILS: HIGH PEAKS REGION
Definitive guide to the High Peaks
Volume I in ADK Forest Preserve Series
GUIDE TO ADIRONDACK TRAILS: NORTHERN REGION
Volume II in ADK Forest Preserve Series
GUIDE TO ADIRONDACK TRAILS: CENTRAL REGION
Volume III in ADK Forest Preserve Series
GUIDE TO ADIRONDACK TRAILS: NORTHVILLE-PLACID TRAIL
Volume IV in ADK Forest Preserve Series
GUIDE TO ADIRONDACK TRAILS: WEST-CENTRAL REGION
Volume V in ADK Forest Preserve Series
GUIDE TO ADIRONDACK TRAILS: EASTERN REGION
Volume VI in ADK Forest Preserve Series
GUIDE TO ADIRONDACK TRAILS: SOUTHERN REGION
Volume VII in ADK Forest Preserve Series
GUIDE TO CATSKILL TRAILS
Volume VIII in ADK Forest Preserve Series
CLIMBING IN THE ADIRONDACKS
A guide to rock and ice routes
ADIRONDACK CANOE WATERS—NORTH FLOW
Over 700 miles of canoe routes in St. Lawrence/
Lake Champlain drainage basins
ADIRONDACK CANOE WATERS—SOUTH AND WEST FLOW
Black River Basin, Mohawk Basin, Upper Hudson
Basin and the two major streams of the Tug Hill Plateau
WINTERWISE
A Backpacker's guide to winter hiking and camping

Price list on request

The ADK Forest Preserve Series

Adirondack
Mountain Club

Compact, durable, hiker-oriented guides recognized as *the source* of Adirondack backcountry information.

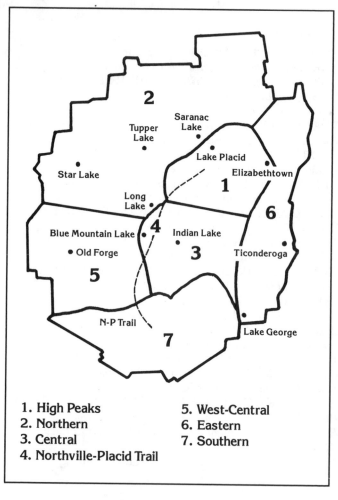

1. High Peaks
2. Northern
3. Central
4. Northville-Placid Trail

5. West-Central
6. Eastern
7. Southern

Each guide contains a 33″ x 20″ topo map.

$12.95 each

Available in bookstores and outdoor equipment stores or from the Adirondack Mountain Club, R.R. 3, Box 3055, Lake George NY 12845-9523 (Tel: 518-668-4447).